Carolina Bride

INSPIRED DESIGN FOR A BESPOKE AFFAIR

This book is available in quantity at special discounts for your group or organization. For further information, contact:

Triumph Books LLC
814 North Franklin
Chicago, Illinois 60610
www.triumphbooks.com

Printed in China.
ISBN: 978-1-62937-020-0
Design by Drew Humphries
Fonts by Laura Worthington

Front and Back Cover Photos © Dréa Cunningham, Photo Artist.
Shot on location in Charleston, SC.
Inside Front Cover Photo by Heather Payne Photography
Inside Back Cover Photo by Laura Gordon Photography

Carolina Bride
The Charlotte Observer, A McClatchy Publication
Publisher, Ann Caulkins
Executive Editor, Sarah Crosland
Editor, Cristina Wilson
Editorial Assistant, Claire Kuhlkin
Although the information in this book has been thoroughly researched, *Carolina Bride* cannot guarantee its accuracy.

Carolina Bride

INSPIRED DESIGN FOR A BESPOKE AFFAIR

Written & Produced *by* Cristina Wilson
Artisic Direction & Design *by* Drew Humphries
Foreword *by* Ceci Johnson

Cover Photos by Dréa Cunningham, Photo Artist • Foreword Photo by Sofia Negron Photography

Title Page Photo by Heather Payne Photography • Introduction Photos by Kristin Vining Photography

TRIUMPH BOOKS, CHICAGO

CONTENTS

 don't want to step on any toes, but I think it's officially time to rethink the stereotype of Southern weddings. Mason jars, burlap, and barns can be lovely, but let's forge a new way and put a fresh, glamorous take on the traditional. Push the boundaries of what's expected and think of your wedding as a beautiful, exciting, artistic expression of who you are as a modern-day couple.

Chances are, if you're reading this book, you may feel the same way, but are seeking a little inspiration or the right direction to get started. Luckily, these pages are filled with drop-dead-gorgeous ideas from flowers, gowns, and even a few of my own invitation designs that I can't wait to reveal here for the first time.

Although I work with clients all over the world, I must say that Southern brides still have a certain charm that is undeniably lovely and warm. They also often have the luxury of beautiful wedding spaces like sprawling lawns, grand estates, or even waterside locales that can lend a great deal of beauty to the day. When considering your wedding design, you can certainly use these as a springboard, but also bring in anything else that makes your heart sing: fashion, design, architecture, travel, art, food… you name it.

What's most important is to be true to yourself and your style as a couple. Take a nod from tradition, but with your own twist. If you fill your day with personal, luxurious, and thoughtful details, guests are sure to feel the signature hospitality! Here's to beautifying your world and many more gorgeous Southern weddings to come.

Cheers!

CELEBRITY DESIGNER
Founder & Creative Director, Ceci New York
Editor, *Ceci Style Magazine*

From the lapping waves and soft sands of the Eastern shoreline to the smoky blue mystique of the mountains dotting our Western borders—and outstretched plains, quaint towns, and bustling urban centers in between—the Carolinas offer almost every imaginable backdrop for the wedding of your dreams.

The artisans who can create a fairy-tale celebration, from the florist who chooses the perfect blooms to the photographer who captures those once-in-a-lifetime memories, range just as widely in style and aesthetic. Whether you seek a traditional affair with natural beauty or an over-the-top luxe soirée, nothing is out of reach.

With this book, it is our mission to share an artful approach to weddings in the new South. Gather round the table for a family-style feast, retreat to a mountain cliff for an elegant elopement, or surprise your guests with a Kelly Wearstler-inspired design for the modern trendsetter. And along the way, we've shared real weddings that exude the joy we hope you experience during this process—real weddings that are thoughtful in design and undeniable celebrations of love.

From two Carolina girls to all of you, congratulations on your happy day. We are grateful to share even a few moments with you during this precious journey. And we're raising our glasses to a beautiful day—and a lifetime of love.

-Cristina & Drew
WRITER & DESIGNER

IN ATTENDANCE

MANOR OF STYLE

 CAKES BY CHLOE
Cake

 HAUSER RENTAL SERVICE
Chairs, China, Flatware & Glassware

 LA TAVOLA
Linens

 LAZARO FROM VICTORIAN ROSE BRIDAL
Gowns

 PALMETTO PEARL
Calligraphy

 PERRY VAILE PHOTOGRAPHY
Photography

 PHOTOVISION
Film Processing

 RACHEL CABLES, MARILYN'S AGENCY
Model

 REBECCA ROSE CREATIVE
Invitation Suite

 REBECCA ROSE EVENTS
Styling, Creative Direction & Floral Design

 SOUND ILLUSIONS
Lighting

 THE BELLA HAIR CO.
Hair & Makeup

 THE GRAYLYN ESTATE
Venue

AMONG THE OAKS

Abany Bauer, Styling & Flowers
Ash & Co, Hair & Makeup
Gossamer, Gowns
Heather Payne Photography, Photography
Leslie Manzano, Tout Talent, Model
Richard Photo Lab, Film Processing
RiverOaks Charleston, Venue

LANIER & SCOTT

Air Haven Limousine, Transportation
Atheneum Creative, Stationery & Paper Goods
Bailey's, Rings and Earrings
Classic Party Rentals, Chairs
Elizabeth Porcher Jones, Calligraphy
Elysium Productions, Cinematography
Ines di Santo from Hannelore's, Gown
Ivy Robinson Events, Wedding Design
J.Crew, Bridesmaids' Dresses
Jami Svay, Hair & Makeup
Jasmine Star, Photography
John Lupton & Andrew Thomas, Floral Design

LANIER & SCOTT CONT.

Johnson C. Smith University, Gospel Choir
JoS. A. Bank Clothiers, Tuxedos
Lynn James & Geraldine Weeks, Food Stylists
Party Crashers, Band
Party Reflections, Tent & Rentals
Party Tables, Custom Draped Tent Liner & Linens
Romona Keveza, Veil
Rusty Guenther, Clergy
Snyder Events, Custom Wood Tent Floor
& Chalkboard Dance Floor
The Art of Cake, Cake
The Inn at Crestwood, Venue

MANOR OF STYLE

The lush grounds and majestic stone of
The Graylyn Estate need no explanation.
Lovely lace and soft candlelight set a
traditional tone of Old World glamour.

Perry Vaile Photography
Rebecca Rose Events
Winston-Salem, NC

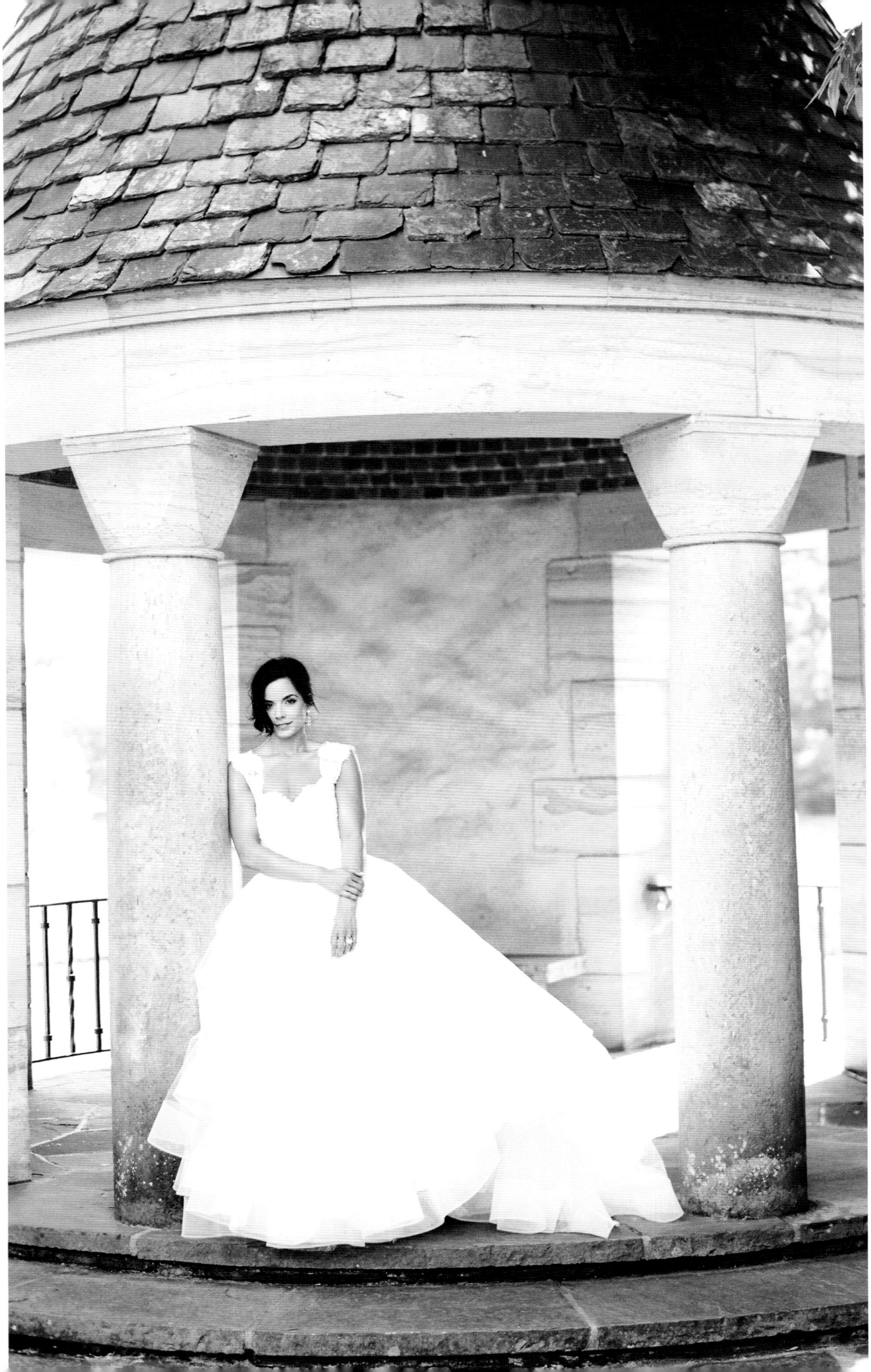

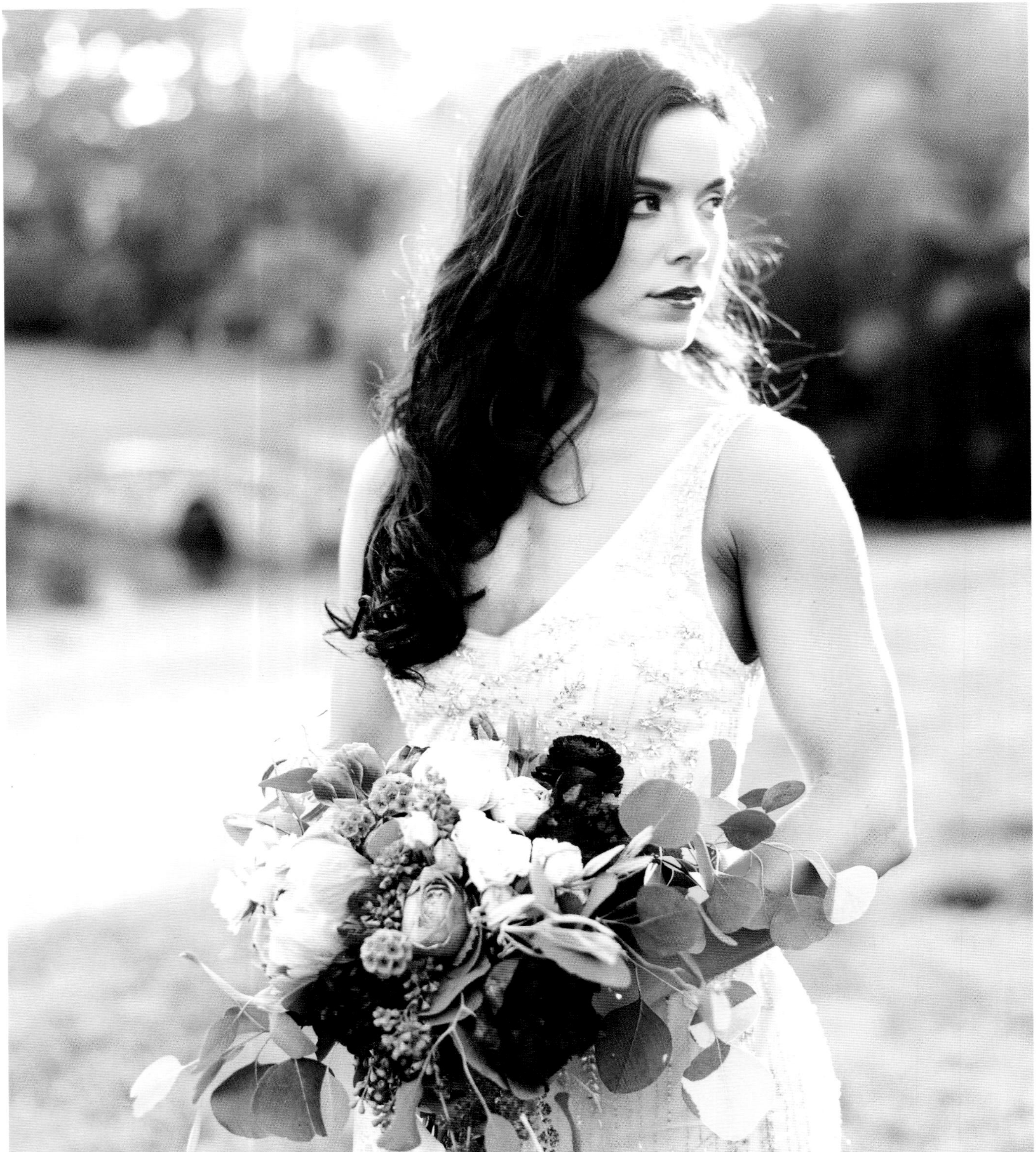

AMONG THE OAKS

Heather Payne Photography

Charleston, SC

LANIER *and* SCOTT

— BLOWING ROCK, NC —

PHOTOGRAPHY BY JASMINE STAR
IVY ROBINSON EVENTS
THE INN AT CRESTWOOD

The Inn at Crestwood is sacred ground, and so much more than a venue, for newlyweds Lanier Swann and Scott Hodgson. Two years prior to their wedding, the bride chose to recover from cancer surgery at her family's vacation home in Blowing Rock; when she felt up to it, she and her parents would dine at Crestwood and savor the sunset. When she fell in love with Scott, and he proposed on Capitol Hill, there was no question that they would celebrate their families in a haven so significant.

The couple drew inspiration from the natural beauty of Blowing Rock for the décor, but very consciously left the details to guru Ivy Robinson. Seeing the lush reception space for the first time—after the ceremony—was an overwhelming experience for the pair, who cherishes their first dance as a life-changing moment. The two danced, and cried, to "Turning Page" by Sleeping at Last, embracing their own new chapter.

*"The first time I took Scott to Blowing Rock, I took him to
Crestwood. There was a wedding going on, and someone took a picture of
us watching the sunset... Exactly one year later we got married there."*

"*I wanted my marriage to be the focus and not the wedding itself. While I focused on the season of engagement and my relationship with Scott, I handed the reins over to Ivy.*"

IN ATTENDANCE

COASTAL LUXE

 42 PRESSED
Paper Suite

 CAROL HANNAH
Wedding Gowns

 CORBIN GURKIN
Photography

 **DOLLY PEARL FROM
BELLA BRIDESMAID
CHARLESTON**
Bridesmaid Dress

 **GATHERING FLORAL
+ EVENT DESIGN,
HEATHER BARRIE
& MARY RUTH TRIBBLE**
Wedding Concept & Design
Floral Arrangements & Specialty Lighting

 **KENDRA SCOTT
FROM BELLA
BRIDESMAID CHARLESTON**
Jewelry

 **LAUREN FETTER,
ELYSIUM AGENCY**
Makeup

 LINDSEY NOWAK
Wardrobe Styling

 **MEG ANN WORKMAN,
ELYSIUM AGENCY**
Hair

 NUAGE DESIGNS
Tablecloth

 **REBECCA BOGGS,
TOUT TALENT**
Model

 RUNNYMEDE PLANTATION
Venue

 SNYDER EVENTS
Furnishings

 **WEDDING CAKES
BY JIM SMEAL**
Cake

 WILDFLOWER LINEN
Overlay

NICHOLE & JASON

7 Once, Band
428 Main Vintage Rentals, "Love" Sign
A Charleston Bride, Melissa Barton,
Wedding Design & Floral Design
Be Pretty, Hair & Makeup
Boone Hall Plantation, Portrait Location
Chaplain Terry Wilson, Clergy
Charleston Black Cab Company, Transportation
Elizabeth Porcher Jones, Calligraphy
Fish Restaurant, Cake & Catering

NICHOLE & JASON CONT.

J.M. Edwards, Rings
KT Merry Photography, Photography
La Tavola, Linens
Men's Wearhouse, Tuxedos
Reem Acra, Gown
Signature Players, Ceremony Music
Snyder Events, Rentals
Studio R Designs, Stationery
The William Aiken House, Venue

PAPER WORK

Ceci New York, Stationery
Corbin Gurkin,
Photography & Styling

KIM & BRODY

Atlanta Showstoppers via East Coast
Entertainment, Band
Cartier, Rings
Diamond Transportation, Transportation
Dr. John Miller, Clergy
Edwin McCain, Reception Music
Herve Leger, Bridesmaids' Dresses
Ivy Robinson Events, Wedding Design
J Major's Bridal Boutique, Veil

KIM & BRODY CONT.

John Lupton & Andrew Thomas, Floral Design
Just Glo Studio, Hair & Makeup
Kristin Vining Photography, Photography
Michael Stanley, Bagpiper
Modern Trousseau from Hayden Olivia Bridal, Gown
Party Tables, Linens
Paul Simon Co., Tuxedos
Ric Standridge, Live Painter
Snyder Events, Rentals
The Cordelle, Cinematography
The Inn at Palmetto Bluff, Venue, Cake & Catering
Voices of Deliverance, Gospel Choir

COASTAL LUXE

*Rich textures and bold metallics meet for a
Charleston soirée under the early autumn sky.*

Photography by Corbin Gurkin
Gathering Floral + Event Design
Charleston, SC

NICHOLE *and* JASON

CHARLESTON, SC

KT MERRY PHOTOGRAPHY
A CHARLESTON BRIDE
THE WILLIAM AIKEN HOUSE

Nichole Smoot and Jason Rapuano knew one thing when they got engaged after a three-year courtship; they would get married in Charleston with an intimate gathering. With ceremony and reception at historic William Aiken House and a portrait session at Boone Hall Plantation, these Southern sweethearts got everything they wished for: a classically elegant celebration bathed in romantic light.

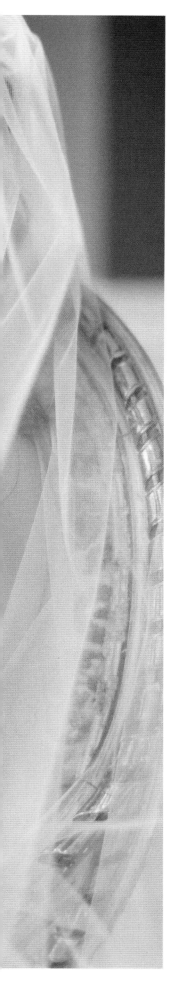

Their 80 guests took in the majestic locale while sipping elderflower and champagne cocktails with fresh raspberries. But the sweetest moment of the day? When the emotion of the ceremony overcame the groom as his lovely bride walked down the aisle.

"It rained so much on our wedding weekend. So much, in fact, that most of historic Charleston flooded the next day! But 30 minutes before the ceremony, the rain stopped and the sun came out, letting us have our ceremony outdoors. The ceremony was truly the sweetest part of the day."

N&
51

From the very first piece of mail—usually the save-the-date—through signs instructing how to bid you farewell, every piece of writing for your wedding should create a world for your guests. Intricate calligraphy adds romantic elegance from a bygone era, and more modern typeface sets the tone for a chic, trendy event. No matter the direction, it's all in the design—a custom brand for your event is the first step in a truly bespoke affair.

KIM *and* BRODY

BLUFFTON, SC

KRISTIN VINING PHOTOGRAPHY
IVY ROBINSON EVENTS
THE INN AT PALMETTO BLUFF

*W*hen a bride and groom want to throw a fabulous party but keep an intimate feel with their very nearest and dearest, they head straight for the iconic Inn at Palmetto Bluff and book the entire idyllic property. Kim Garrison and Brody Glenn did just that, exchanging vows in the Lowcountry surrounded by 100 guests. With a gospel choir, the Atlanta Showstoppers, and songwriter Edwin McCain performing throughout the events, the weekend was all about making a joyful noise.

IN ATTENDANCE

FARMER'S SUPPER

 ANNA NAPHTALI
Styling & Photography

 BOHEMIAN INK
Calligraphy & Hand-lettering

 CECELIA JOHNSON
Model

 CHEF ALYSSA GORELICK
Menu Creation & Cuisine

 CLAIRE PETTIBONE FROM J MAJOR'S BRIDAL BOUTIQUE
Gown (62)

 ERIN ASHLEY MAKEUP
Makeup

 GOLDMINE JOURNAL
Styling, Cake & Favors

 HEY LOVE! EVENTS, GINGER HUSSEY
Wedding Design

 JOHN METCALFE
Model

 NEIMAN MARCUS
Shoes

 NEW YORK BRIDE & GROOM
Gown (64)

 PARTY REFLECTIONS
Farm Tables, Chairs & Flatware

 PHILOSOPHY FLOWERS
Floral Design

 SIMPLY BEAUTIFUL ARTISTRY
Hair

THE PLAID PENGUIN
Food Coordination

TRUE PIZZA
Menu Creation & Cuisine

WEST ELM CHARLOTTE
Serveware & Dishes

QUEEN OF THE FIELDS

Annie Konduros, Evolution Talent Agency, Model
Be Pretty, Hair & Makeup
Bluebird Hill Farm, Venue
Carol Hannah, Gowns (71,72)
Catherine Marciniak Photography, Photography
Kristin Hayes Jewelry, Jewelry & Headpiece
Leanne Marshall, Gown (68)
Richard Photo Lab, Film Processing
Springvine Design, Floral Design

KRISTEN & TIMOTHY

Air Haven Limo, Transportation
All About You, Hair
All Occasions Party Rental, Church Pews
Atheneum Creative, Stationery
Bella Bridesmaids, Bridesmaids' Dresses
Big Ray and the Kool Kats via East Coast
Entertainment, Band
Come+Together Events, Katrina Hutchins,
Wedding Design
Diamonds Direct, Rings
Hermès, Ties
Ink Spot Crow, Cinematography
Jimmy Choo, Shoes
JoS. A. Bank Clothiers, Tuxedos
Lynn Stall, Clergy
Norman Love Confections, Favors
Oriental Trading, Paper Lanterns
Oscar de la Renta from Mark Ingram

Atelier, Gown
Party Reflections, Rentals
Party Tables, Draping & Linens
Royal Rides, Transportation
Split Second Sound, DJ
The Bloom Room, Floral Design
The Eseeola Lodge, Venue & Catering
The Schultzes, Photography
Who's the Fairest, Makeup
Wing Haven Gardens, Portrait Location
Wow Factor Cakes, Cake

FARMER'S SUPPER

Gather round for the freshest fare in a celebration of a working farm's bounty. A Tuscan bruschetta bar simply whets the appetite for whole roasted red snapper, Moroccan lamb shanks, and more. After an evening dancing under the stars, brick oven baked craft pizzas finish the feast.

Styling & Photography by Anna Naphtali
Wedding Design by Hey Love! Events
Food Coordination by The Plaid Penguin
Waxhaw, NC

charlotte
mason
6 MEADOW LANE APT #23
CHARLOTTE NC 28210

kindly reply
by m
ouch july to
with joy
or with regrets

florence and matthew
request the pleasure of
your company at their
wedding on august 29, 2014
at five o'clock in the evening
2650 newtown road waxhaw nc
28117

florence bland
4 4 o meadow en.
charlotte nc
28210

margaret
billings

new lolly farms

ceremony

QUEEN OF THE FIELDS

Catherine Marciniak Photography

Bennett, NC

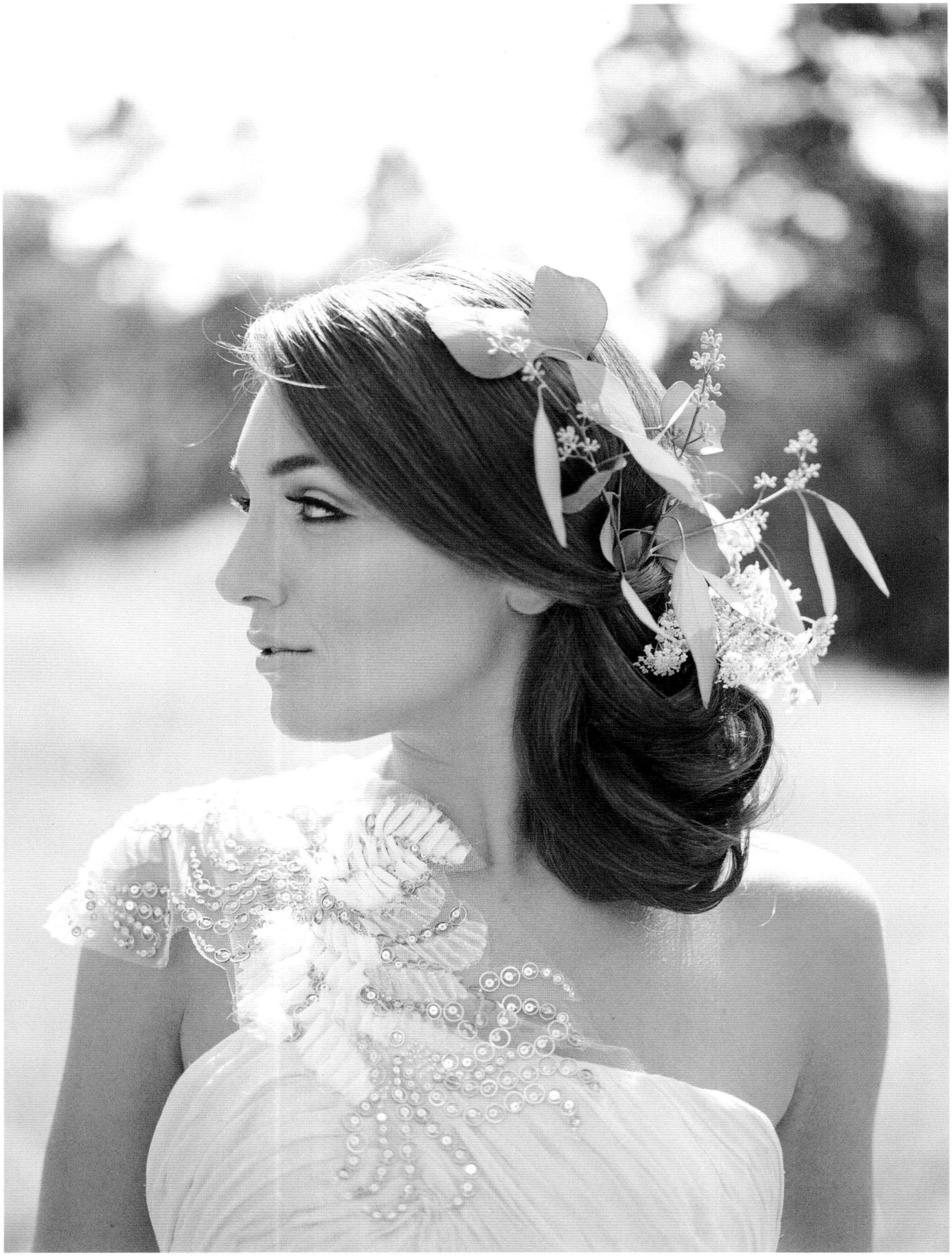

KRISTEN *and* TIMOTHY

LINVILLE, NC

PHOTOGRAPHY BY THE SCHULTZES
COME+TOGETHER EVENTS
THE ESEEOLA LODGE

Bride Kristen Cone grew up in Blowing Rock and knew she would wed someday in the majestic North Carolina Mountains. Her Eseeola wedding to Timothy Snead, however, was anything but rustic, with an Hermès bracelet as the muse for the lavender and navy color palette; an Hermès tie in the same hues inspired the modern geometric motif in the stationery. And decisiveness preceded this couple before they had to choose the décor: the pair enjoyed a whirlwind courtship of just six months before tying the knot.

"When I pulled up to the
tent with my mom, to the actual
ceremony site, it was overwhelming.
I saw the church pews and the
altar that we had made, and
I thought—this is real."

IN ATTENDANCE

GARDEN VARIETY

 A FISHERMAN'S WIFE
China

 BRENT HOLLOMAN DESIGNS
Invitation

 HARBORSIDE EVENT RENTALS
Table

 **HIGH PERFORMANCE LIGHTING**
Lighting

 **J.CREW**
Suit

 JOY NOELLE
Gown

 KC ALLISON & DANA WHITE
Bride & Groom

 MILLIE HOLLOMAN PHOTOGRAPHY MILLIE & AMANDA HOLLOMAN
Photography

 ONE BELLE BAKERY
Cake

 PARTY SUPPLIERS AND RENTALS
Linens

PRESSED COTTON
Brown Bottles & Guest Book

 RICHARD PHOTO LAB
Film Processing

 SALON FRINGE
Hair & Makeup

 SALT HARBOR DESIGNS, JENNIFER ROSE
Styling & Flowers

 SOUTHERN BEE DESIGNS
Calligraphy

 THE ATRIUM BY LIGON FLYNN
Venue

JODI & JOHN

Absolutely Charleston, Transportation
Bourbon and Boweties, Custom, Bridesmaids' Jewelry
Charleston Tuxedo, Groomsmen's Tuxedos
East West Productions, Cinematography
Fish Restaurant, Catering
French Huguenot Church, Ceremony
Gathering Floral + Event Design,
Floral Design & Custom Furnishings
Groovetown, Band
Henri Daussi, Engagement Ring
Hugo Boss, Groom's Tuxedo
Jenny Packham, Headpiece
Kate Spade, Shoes
Kristin Newman Designs, Wedding Planner & Design
Lowndes Grove Plantation, Venue
Meg Ann Workman, Wedding Hair by Charlotte, Hair & Makeup
Oscar and Emma Custom Design Studio, Stationery
Rev. Thomas Guerry, Clergy

Snyder Events, Rentals
Suwa, Rings
Technical Event Company, Specialty Lighting
Timwill Photography, Tim Willoughby, Photography
Vera Wang from Alexia's Bridal, Gown & Veil
Wedding Cakes by Jim Smeal, Cake

TO HAVE & TO HOLD

Corbin Gurkin, Photography
Lily Greenthumb's Wedding & Event
Design, Bouquets
Separk Mansion, Venue

ELIZABETH & SPENCER

Brownlee Jewelers, Rings
Charlotte Cake Man, Cake
DeLane Hayes, DJ
Executive Car Service, Transportation
J.Crew, Groom's Suit
Lauren Rosenau Photography, Photography

Lela Rose, Bridesmaids' Dresses
Lyssa Whitson & Brenda Scott, Musicians
New York Bride & Groom, Veil
Nichole Smith, Hair & Makeup
Rev. Barbara Barden, Clergy
Shirley Hilburn, Wedding Coordinator
Studio His & Hers, Mixbook, Stationery
The Victorian Crow's Nest, Venue & Catering
Trudy Green, Floral Design & Headpiece

GARDEN VARIETY

Dusty turquoise, yellow, and apricot with touches of copper shine create a warm glow in this secret garden locale. European courtyard meets contemporary cool for an intimate celebration.

Millie Holloman Photography
Salt Harbor Designs
Wilmington, NC

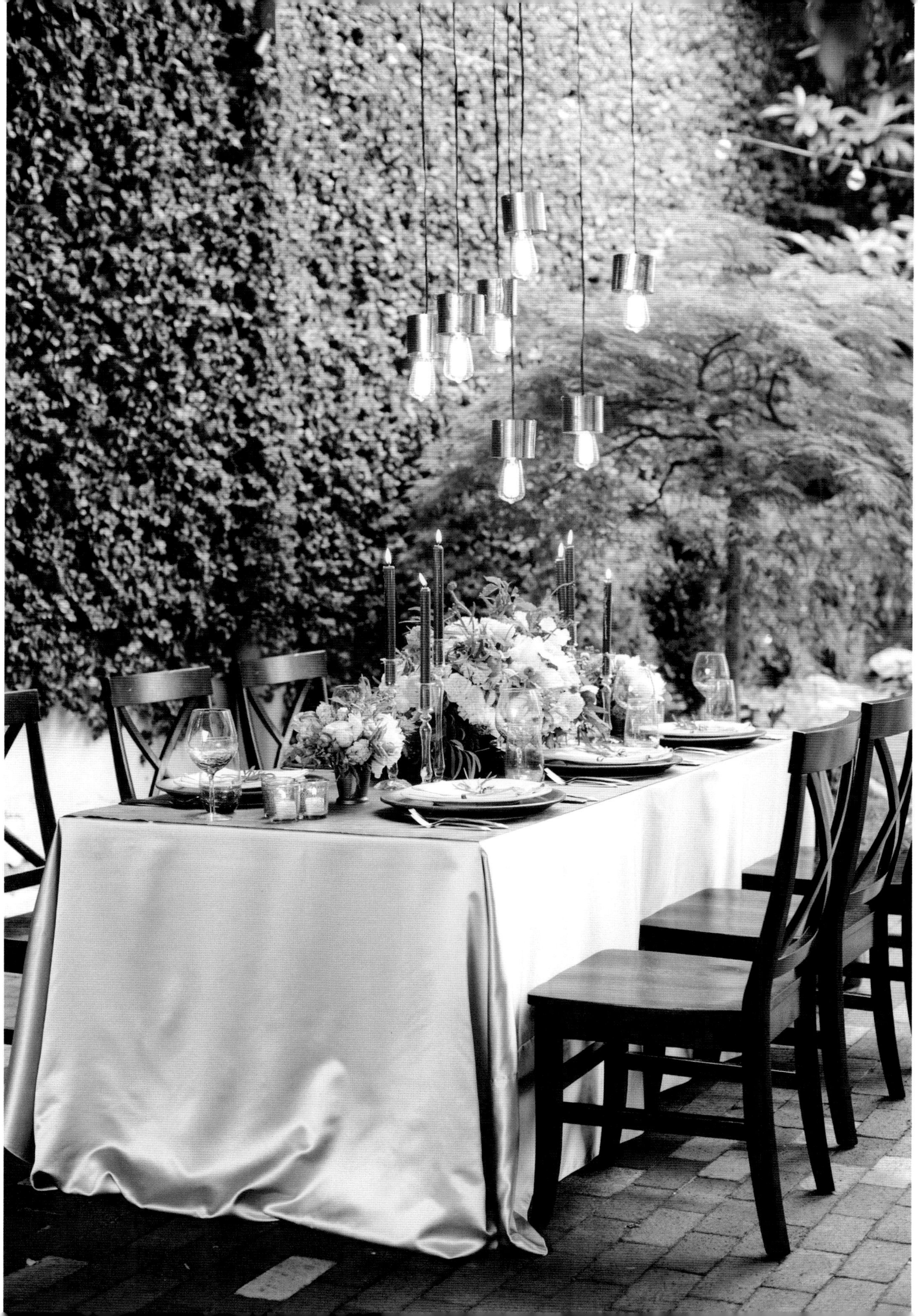

JODI *and* JOHN

— CHARLESTON, SC —

TIMWILL PHOTOGRAPHY
KRISTIN NEWMAN DESIGNS
LOWNDES GROVE PLANTATION

After three years of long-distance courtship, Jodi Heyens and John Strenkowski, and guests from across the globe, convened in Charleston for a wedding weekend under the stars. Drawing inspiration from her native Canada's wine country, Jodi collaborated with Kristin Newman Designs on organic décor with Tuscan flair. It's no wonder the bride appreciates simple elegance and letting a beautiful place speak for itself— she's now the owner of her own historic wedding venue, The Merrimon-Wynne House in Raleigh, NC. And as any Southerner can appreciate, the two celebrated their permanent homecoming to Raleigh with Old Crow Medicine Show's "Wagon Wheel," a first dance full of soul.

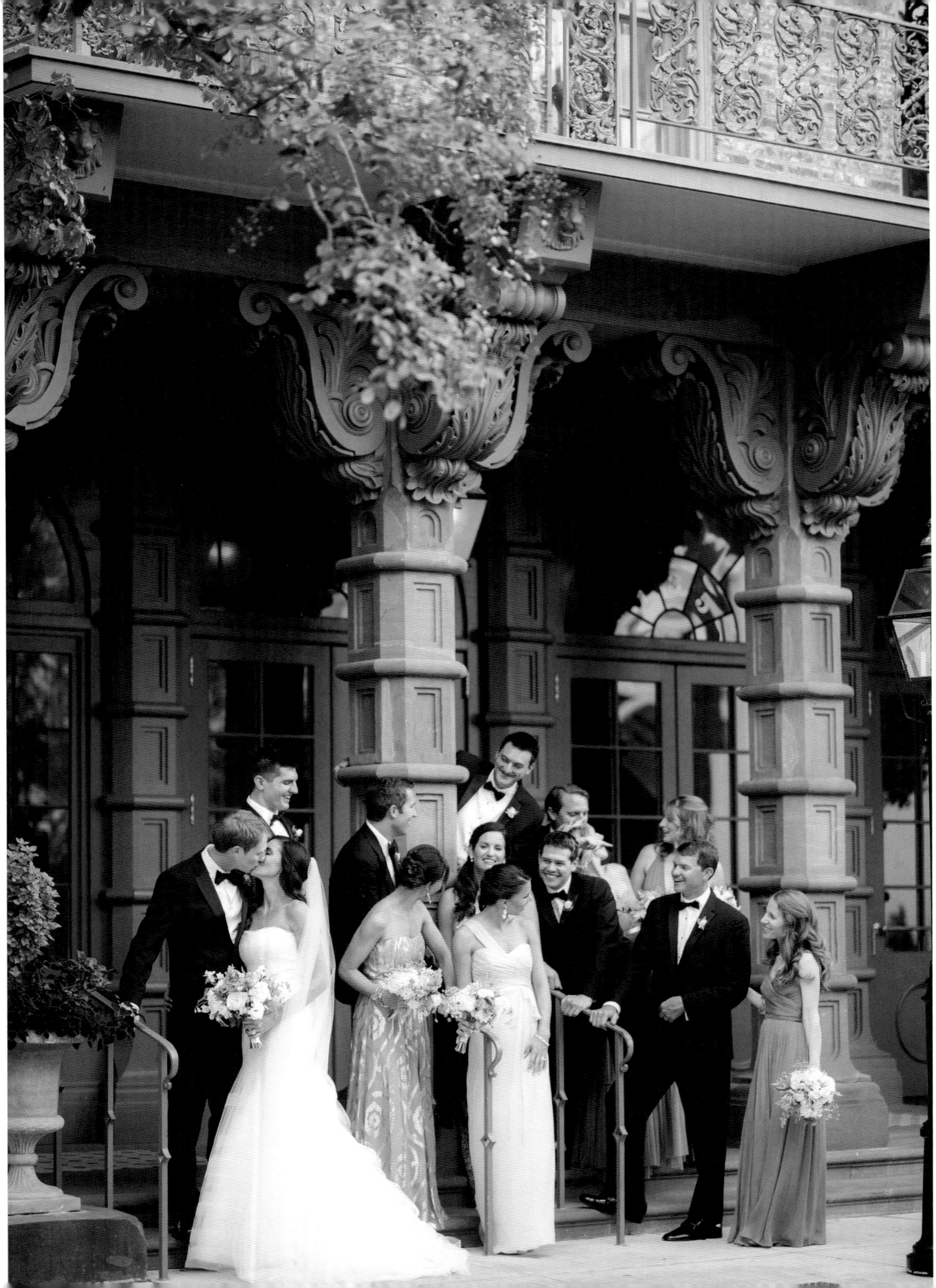

"We wanted our guests to feel like they were at a beautiful family meal, dining under the stars at a vineyard in wine country."

To have and to hold

Your arm is intertwined with your father's, the music begins to play, and you start the walk down the aisle toward a newly shared life. Your bouquet is a symbolic and poignant part of that moment, and can't be overlooked. Traditional blooms include roses, lilies, and peonies, but orchids and ranunculus are also fresh choices for an elegant bridal look. You may wish to incorporate specific blooms to represent the important women in your life, or choose flowers with a sentimental tie to your courtship.

ELIZABETH *and* SPENCER

MONROE, NC

LAUREN ROSENAU PHOTOGRAPHY
THE VICTORIAN CROW'S NEST

*S*ipping champagne in a lavender scented, clawfoot-tub bath right before the ceremony sums up bride Elizabeth Arzani's wedding journey—relaxed, vintage, and effortlessly beautiful. Elizabeth and fiancé Spencer Gaddy created a whimsical oasis for their guests, from over-sized paper flowers to birdcage centerpieces to wildflower bouquets. With the bride—a mixed media artist—in her mother's debutante dress and great grandmother's vintage jewels and the 'maids in vibrant gowns with flowers tucked behind their ears, the wedding party itself reflected the *joie de vivre* felt by all.

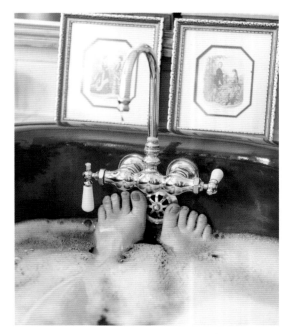

"I'm a mixed media artist so I used the wedding as an excuse to collect things I loved and think, how could I use that later? I already had a collection of birdcages, so I wanted to continue that... I always knew since I was young that I wanted to wear my mom's dress."

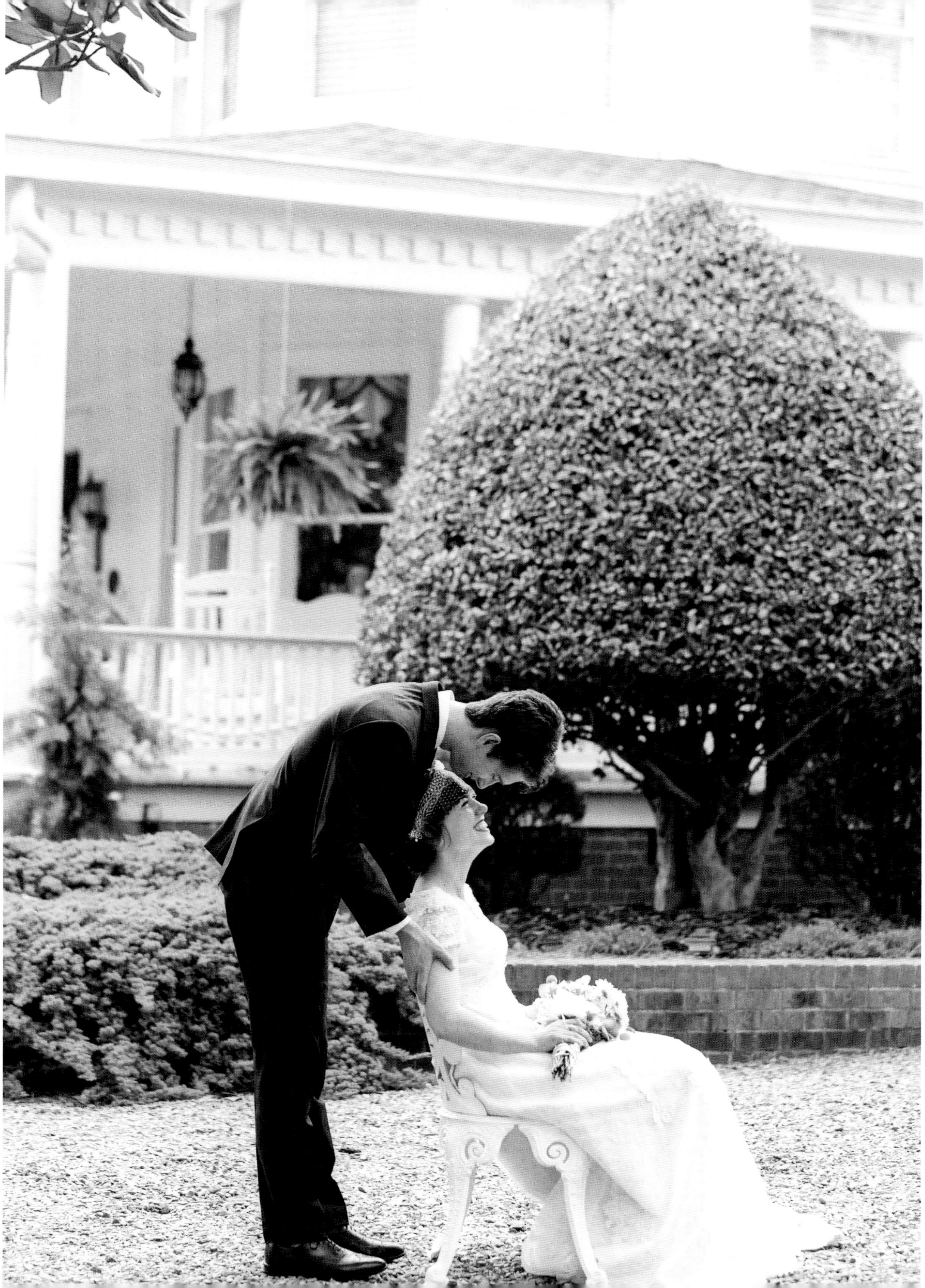

IN ATTENDANCE

NEW SOUTH LOVE

A DARLING DAY
Vintage Rentals

ANGELA COX
Photography

ANGIE & JONATHAN THOMPSON
Bride & Groom

ART EATS BAKERY
Cake

BELLE MAQUILLAGE
Makeup

CHRISTINA NICOLE
Necklace, Stacking Rings,
Groom's Ring, Earrings

DARK CORNER DISTILLERY MOONSHINE
Cocktail

GREENBRIER FARMS
Location

HEATHER COX
Hair

MILK MOON
Wardrobe Styling

MOE MEGAN
Creative Direction & Styling

PONTHIEUX'S JEWELRY DESIGN STUDIO
Engagement Ring

STATICE FLORAL COUTURE
Floral Design & Styling

STUDIO SARAHROSE
Invitation, Lettering & Cake Painting

SWAMP RABBIT GROCERY
Food

STRIKING BEAUTY

Adriana Flores Felder, Bride
Dr. Josephus W. Hall House & Salisbury Railway Passenger Station;
Historic Salisbury Foundation, Venues
Jimmy Choo, Shoes
La Familia, Headpiece (109)
Laura James Jewelry, Jewelry
Nectar Floral Designs, Floral Design
Parker J Photography (106, 110-112), Photography
Richard Israel (107-109, 113), Photography
Sara Egri, Hair & Makeup
Ship to Shore, Gowns & Veil

MONIKA & AAKAR

AFR Furniture Rental, Rentals
Blossoms at Biltmore Park, Floral Design and Mandap
Blue Nile, Rings
Carolina Carriage Company, Horse & Carriage
Dilip Gore, Clergy
DJ Rang, DJ
Dollbox Productions, Makeup
Jimmy Choo, Shoes
Kristin Byrum Photography, Photography
Maharani Indian Cuisine, Catering
My Shadi Cards, Stationery
Rex Yau, Cinematography
Suraj Spa & Salon, Hair
The Crest Center and Pavilion, Venue
Tiffany's Baking Co., Cake
Shutterbooth, Photo Booth

NEW SOUTH LOVE

Inspired by the intoxicating hellebore flower, rugged textures and naturally vibrant hues evoke nostalgia for rich, Southern tradition. Local collards, freshly pulled carrots, and sweet peaches are found alongisde antlers and jagged wood: the South's resilient grit and beauty on display.

Angela Cox Photography
Creative Direction & Styling by Moe Megan
Easley, SC

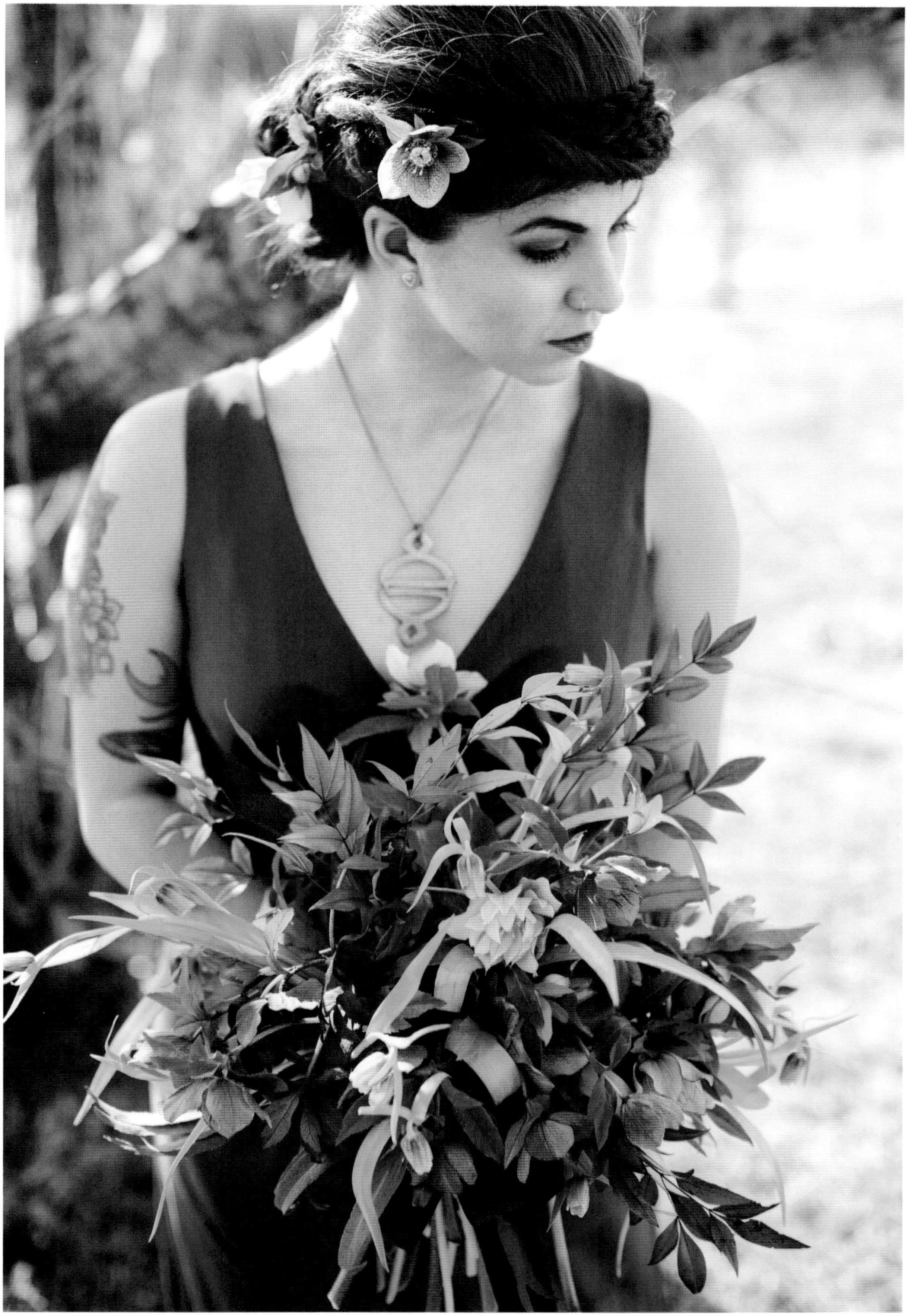

Love
is enough though
the World
be a waning &
the woods have
no voice but the
voice of complaining
though the sky
be too dark for
dim eyes to discover
the gold cups &
daisies fair blooming
there under though
the hills be
dark shadows &
the sea a
dark wonder &
this day draw
a veil over all
deeds pass'd over
Yet their hands
shall not tremble
their feet
shall not falter
the void
shall not weary
the fear shall not alter
these lips & these eyes
of the loved &
the Lover

Poem by William Morris

STRIKING BEAUTY

Richard Israel & Parker J Photography

Salisbury, NC

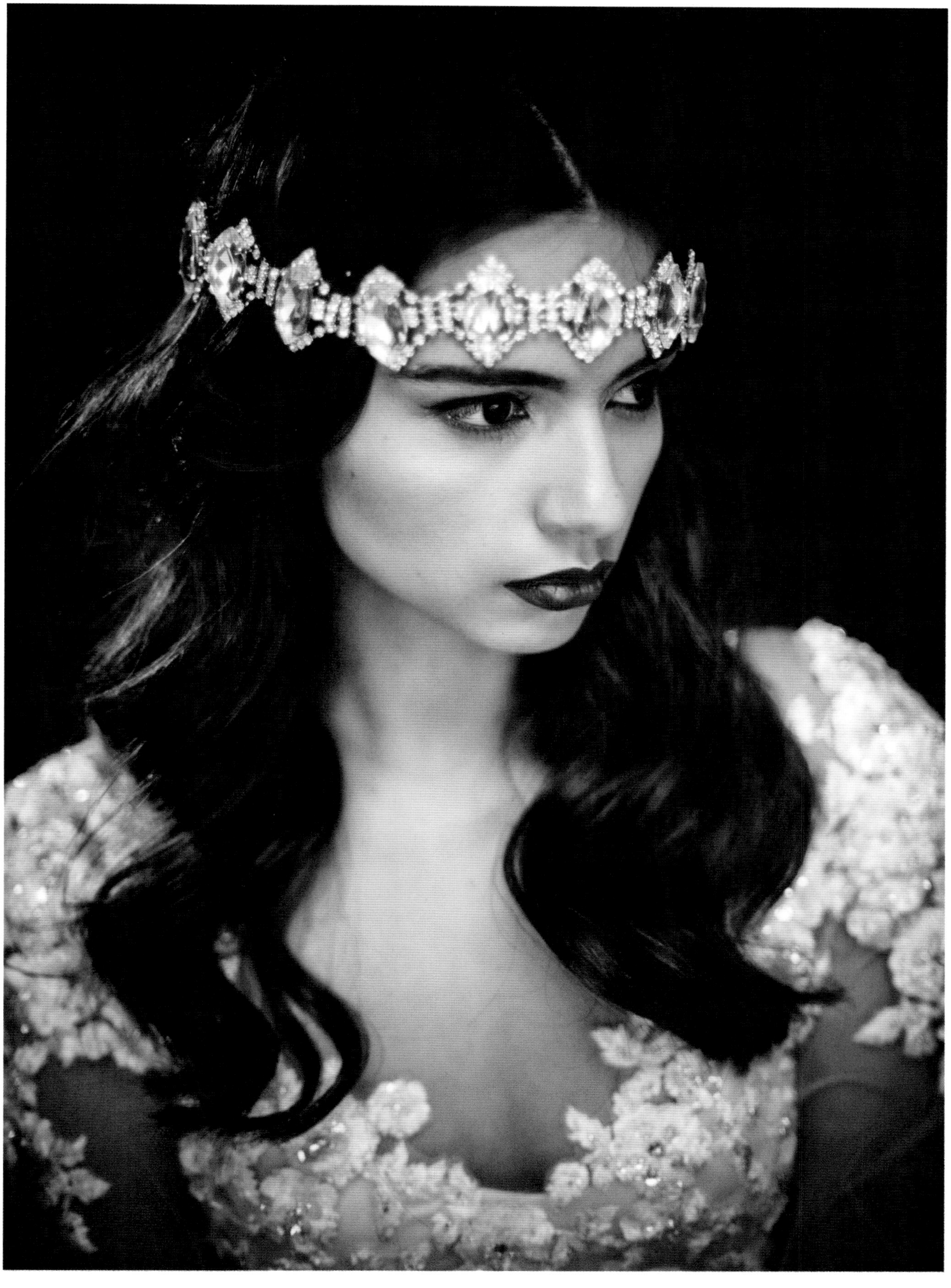

MONIKA *and* AAKAR

ASHEVILLE, NC

KRISTIN BYRUM PHOTOGRAPHY
THE CREST CENTER & PAVILION

Traditional Indian weddings are known for their lengthy festivities and even lengthier guest lists, but for Monika Gondha and Aakar Vachhani, it was all about personal twists on tradition. Instead of a celebration in hometown Charlotte, the bride sought an unusual outdoor space that could accommodate her 300-person party. The Crest Center provided the perfect backdrop, and even the weather had a few surprises in store for them. A misty mountain fog rolled in during the start of Saturday's festivities, but just before the couple wed under an ivory and purple mandap, the skies cleared for the majestic, open-air ceremony.

"In an Indian wedding, the groom gets to the ceremony site first, and his view is blocked with a white sheet while the bride comes down the aisle and sits... When they dropped the sheet and I was sitting there across from him, it hit me. This is real, I'm getting married."

"My father suddenly and unexpectedly passed away just a few months before the wedding... It was a happy and sad day at the same time. My mom gave an amazing speech—probably the first time in her life she's given a speech—and seeing her so strong, I will always remember that moment."

Work of art

PHOTOGRAPHY THAT SPEAKS TO THE SOUL

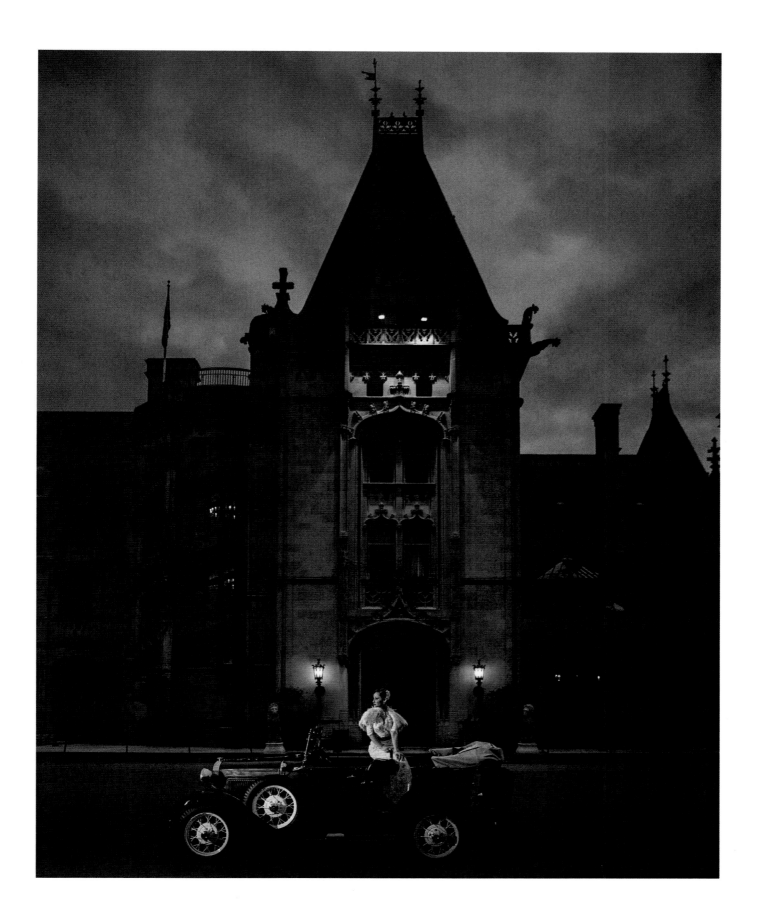

IN ATTENDANCE

IN ATTENDANCE

MODERN ICON

 ANDRASSY CUSTOM CONSTRUCTION
Custom Bench Swing

 ATHENEUM CREATIVE
Invitation, Escort Cards & Menu Design

 CE RENTAL
Flatware

 ISABELLE ARMSTRONG
Gown (150)

 IVY ROBINSON EVENTS
Event Design & Styling

 KELLY ODOM FLOWERS
Floral Design

 KELLY WEARSTLER
China

 KRISTIN HAYES JEWELRY
Jewelry

 LIANCARLO FROM ALEXIA'S BRIDAL
Gown (153)

 MARY MAC VINTAGE
Vintage, Lucite, & Brass Chairs, Marble Dining Table

 MILLIE HOLLOMAN PHOTOGRAPHY, MILLIE & AMANDA HOLLOMAN
Photography

 MONAÉ ELLIS
Model

 MYERS MCKENZIE
Hair

 PRIVATE RESIDENCE, COURTESY OF AUBRE & JOSH VAUGHN
Venue

 TERI-LYN MAKEUP ARTIST
Makeup

 WOW FACTOR CAKES
Cake & Desserts

LET THERE BE LIGHT

Corbin Gurkin, Photography
Ivy Robinson Events,
Design & Lighting

SOU & JOSH

Artisan Ice Sculptures, Ice Bars
Belk Chapel at Queens University, Ceremony
Crystal Stokes Photography, Photography
Dean Vong, Officiant
Diamonds Direct, Rings
Erin Ashley Makeup, Makeup
Fahrenheit Restaurant, Portrait Venue
Ginger Wyrick & Emily Chatham, Musicians
Greene Leaf Productions, Cinematography
Holiday Inn, Laotian Ceremony Venue
Inbal Dror from Joan Pillow Salon, Gown
Original Runner Co., Aisle Runner

SOU & JOSH CONT.

Party Reflections, Rentals
Peak Limousine, Transportation
Planned Perfection, Angela Recinella, Wedding Design
Rebekah McCann, Hair
Split Second Sound, DJ
Strike-A-Pose, Photo Booth
The Flower Diva, Floral Design
The Ritz-Carlton, Charlotte, Reception Venue,
Catering & Cake
Three Little Birds, Stationery

MODERN ICON

Fall into a Kelly Wearstler-inspired world of black marble, eclectic gold, and whimsical pattern. With minimalist florals and rocker-glam jewels, an ultra-chic affair is right at your fingertips.

Millie Holloman Photography
Ivy Robinson Events
Raleigh, NC

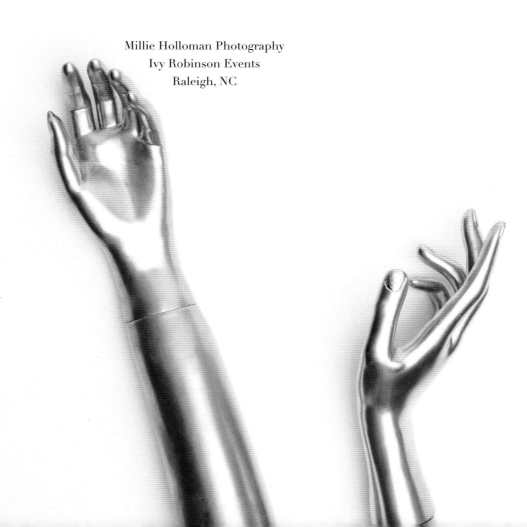

Let there be light

You've walked down the aisle and the vows have been exchanged.
Now it's time for your guests to experience everything you've
planned for them. Nothing sets the tone for an unforgettable event
like the perfect glow. With soft, romantic candlelight, a sleek, modern fixture, or perhaps a castle-worthy chandelier, the most beautiful
table in the world wouldn't be complete without the delicate balance
of light and shadow.

SOU *and* JOSH

CRYSTAL STOKES PHOTOGRAPHY
PLANNED PERFECTION
THE RITZ-CARLTON, CHARLOTTE

The best things come in threes, or at least that's the case for Sou Chanhthirath and Josh Astete when they reflect on their chic, uptown Charlotte wedding. The couple had three goals for the weekend: to embrace their respective traditions, to provide an incredible reunion for family and friends long separated, and to throw an unforgettable dance party.

They succeeded on all accounts, incorporating their Peruvian, Laotian, and American roots into a weekend that blended welcoming warmth and beautiful details.

"I knew that I wanted to wear Spanish lace, but I was torn between a ball gown and a mermaid style dress. ... [The Inbal Dror gown] had everything I was looking for. It gave me the wow factor but was also understated, elegant yet sexy, and it made me feel like a princess."

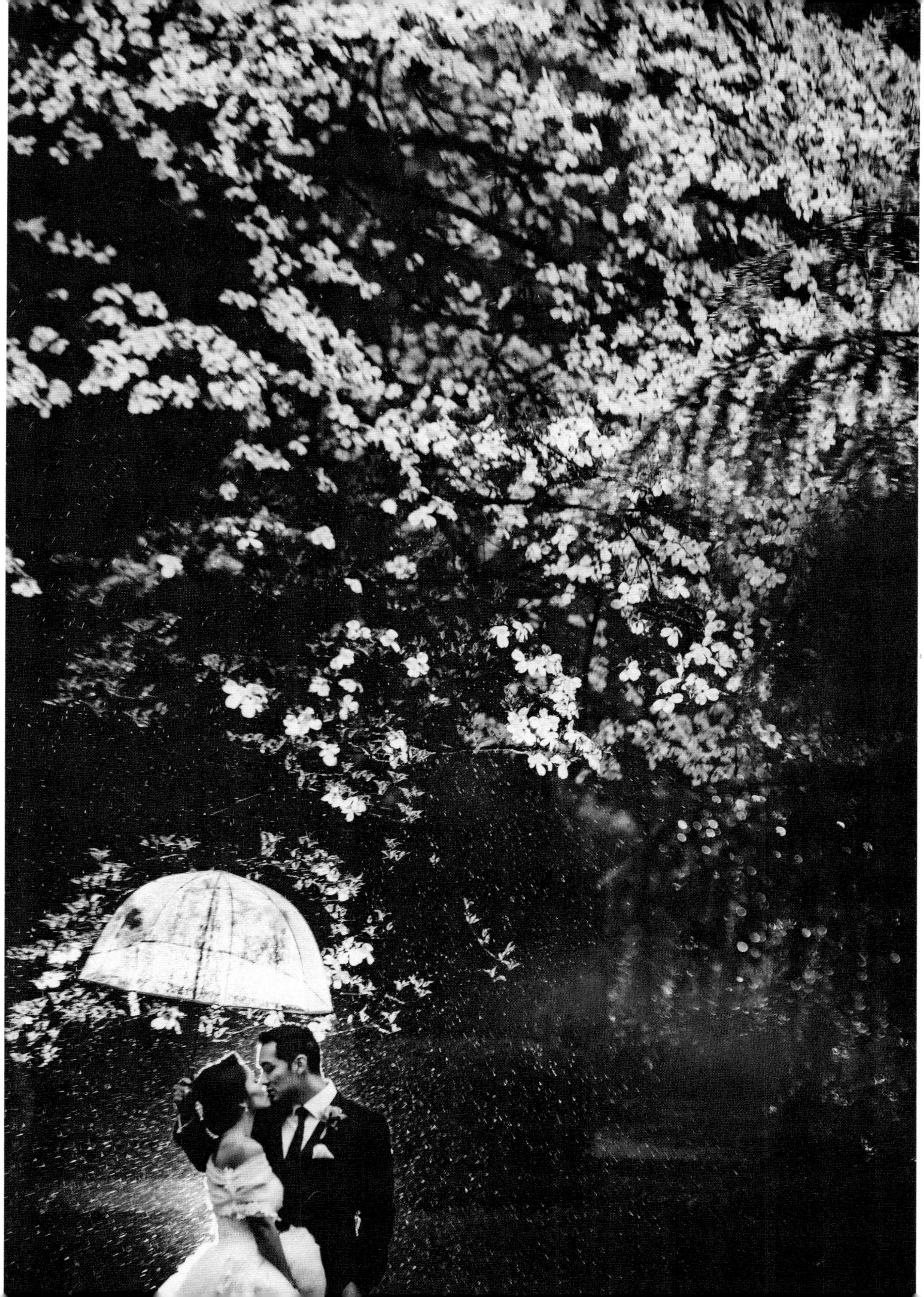

IN ATTENDANCE

BOHEMIAN BEAUTY

 CRYSTAL STOKES PHOTOGRAPHY
Photography

 ERIN ASHLEY MAKEUP
Makeup

 HALIE BIGGS
Model

 J MAJOR'S BRIDAL BOUTIQUE
Gown (165)

 MIRROR BOMB STUDIO
Hair

 NEW CREATIONS FLOWER COMPANY
Floral Design

 PARTY REFLECTIONS
Woven Chargers & Flatware

 PINK TOAST INK
Paper Goods

 SCOUT & MOLLY'S
Jewelry (164)

 SOMETHING CLASSIC CATERING & CAFES
Food & Beverage

 THE ESEEOLA LODGE, LINVILLE, NC
Venue

 THE GRACEFUL HOST, ASHLEY CASH
Wedding Design & Styling

 UPPER BARN RENTALS
Farm Table & Furniture Rentals

 WORLD MARKET, SLEEPY POET ANTIQUE MALL & THE DEPOT AT GIBSON MILL
Collected Décor Items

 WOW FACTOR CAKES
Cake & Desserts

 ZUHAIR MURAD
Gown & Belt (164)

DAUGHTERS OF THE WATER

Abigail Johnson, Sophia LaVecchia & Melina Daniels, Models
Anna Naphtali, Photography
Bailey Plantation House, Wedding Venue
Bohemian Ink, Headpieces
Dannon K. Collard, Makeup
Egrets Pointe Townhouses, Travel Venue
Pastel Makeup & Hair, Hair
Samuelle Couture, Gowns

JESSIE & JEFF

Alaia from Bridal House of Charleston, Gown
Bridal House of Charleston, Veil
Buy the Bunch, Floral Design
Capelli Salon, Hair & Makeup
Delphine Press, Stationery
JoS. A. Bank Clothiers, Tuxedos
Julia Badgett, Clergy
Lee Edwards Entertainment, Entertainment
Moseley's Diamond Showcase, Rings
Relish Distinctive Catering, Catering, Rentals & Coordination
Ride It Out, Transportation
Sash Bridesmaid Boutique, Bridesmaids' Dresses
Seychelles, Shoes
The Pavilion at Patriots Point, Venue
Tiers of Joy, Cake
We Are the Hoffmans, Photography

BOHEMIAN BEAUTY

Invite guests to gather for an evening of effortless elegance under the stars. The spirit of the mountains speaks through this laid-back take on boho-chic. It's all about the love.

Crystal Stokes Photography
The Graceful Host
Linville, NC

DAUGHTERS
OF THE
WATER

Photography by Anna Naphtali

Edisto Island, SC

JESSIE  JEFF

— MT. PLEASANT, SC —

PHOTOGRAPHY BY WE ARE THE HOFFMANS
PATRIOTS POINT

For spunky bride Jessie Mahney with her blush gown and poppy lips, the entertainment drove the ambiance of her Charleston wedding to Jeff Badgett. A lifelong love of music and dancing made song selection for the big day of the utmost importance, and every choice embraced the message of lasting love and family. For Jessie's first dance with her father, she selected "Tiny Dancer" by Elton John, a favorite for the pair and a surprise from the bride until the big moment. And if the surprise wasn't emotional enough, Jeff and his mother joined in halfway through, and by the end of the song the entire bridal party was belting every lyric. With a deep connection to the water, the couple knew the salty air and vivid sunset of Patriots Point was the perfect backdrop for their lyrical romance.

"I wanted my lips to be the color they are when you come inside from being in the cold."

IN ATTENDANCE

NAUTICAL CHIC

 ANNA BAGINSKI
Model

 ASHLEY BROOK PERRYMAN
Hair & Makeup

 CALLIE WHITE
Signature Cocktail, Food Trays,
Dessert Forks & Silver Tray

 CHARLESTON STEMS
Floral Design, Salt & Pepper Shakers

 CHRIS NEWMAN
Menu Knots

 CROGHAN'S JEWELERS
Carolina Cups

 DAVID DABNEY
Boat & Driver

 ELIZABETH PORCHER JONES
Calligraphy & Place Cards

 ELIZABETH STUART DESIGN
Chairs

 FAST FOTO AND DIGITAL
Film Processing

 GAP
T-Shirts & Scarf

 GAYLE BROOKER
Photography

 JIMMY CHOO
Shoes

 **KRISTIN NEWMAN,
KRISTIN NEWMAN DESIGNS**
Wedding Design & Styling
Napkins, Place Card Holders, Credenza

 LA TAVOLA
Linens

 **LINDSEY NOWAK FOR
KRISTIN NEWMAN DESIGNS**
Fashion Stylist

 LULAKATE
Gown (184) and Skirt (188)

 **MEGAN BRADLEY FOR
KRISTIN NEWMAN DESIGNS**
Invitation Design

 POTTERY BARN
Chargers & Punch Bowl

 **PRIVATE RESIDENCE,
MT. PLEASANT, SC**
Venue

 SNYDER EVENTS
Stemware & Table

 SUGAR BAKESHOP
Cake & Cupcakes

 UNIQUE TABLE TOP RENTALS
Silverware

 WEDGWOOD STERLING
China & Dessert Plates

SET THE TABLE

Ashley Baber Weddings, Ashley Baber & Erica Stawick,
Design & Styling
Belk, China
Corbin Gurkin, Photography
Lily Greenthumb's Wedding & Event Design, Floral Design
Party Reflections, Linen & Flatware
Separk Mansion, Venue

KARA & JUSTIN

A Floral Affair, Floral Design
All About Me, Bridal Party Hair
Anne Barge from Belle Vie Bridal Couture, Gown
Bella Bridesmaids, Bridesmaids' Dresses
Belle Vie Bridal Couture, Veil
Bill Peterson, Piano
Colleton River Plantation Club, Venue
David Yurman, Groom's Band
Donna Von Bruening Photographers, Photography
Dr. Martin Lifer, Officiant
Emily McCarthy, Stationery
Falcon Fireworks, Fireworks
FX Limousine, Transportation
Hautelocks provided by Spencer Special Events, Bridal Hair
Jimmy Choo, Shoes
JoS. A. Bank Clothiers, Groomsmen's Tuxedos

KARA & JUSTIN CONT.

Kelly Tours, Transportation
Life Stage Films, Cinematography
Maria Elena, Headpiece
Nina Rodman, Organist and Strings Coordinator
Party Tables, Custom Linen & Draping
Providence Presbyterian Church, Ceremony
Radcliffe Jewelers, Bride's Band
Ranco Tent Rentals, Tent
Saks Fifth Avenue, Groom's Tuxedo
Savannah Custom Cakes, Cake
SKINZIN, Makeup
Spencer Special Events,
Wedding Design & Coordination
Technical Event Company, Lighting
The Diamond Room, Engagement Ring
The Maxx via East Coast Entertainment, Band

NAUTICAL CHIC

*Avant-garde meets anchors aweigh with a
fresh take on classic Charleston style. Timeless
navy and cheery yellow weave through preppy
details, from the first hors d'oeuvre to a
glamorous farewell by boat.*

Photography by Gayle Brooker
Kristin Newman Designs
Mt. Pleasant, SC

Miss Katherine Mitchell
Eight Longitude Lane
Charleston, South Carolina
29401

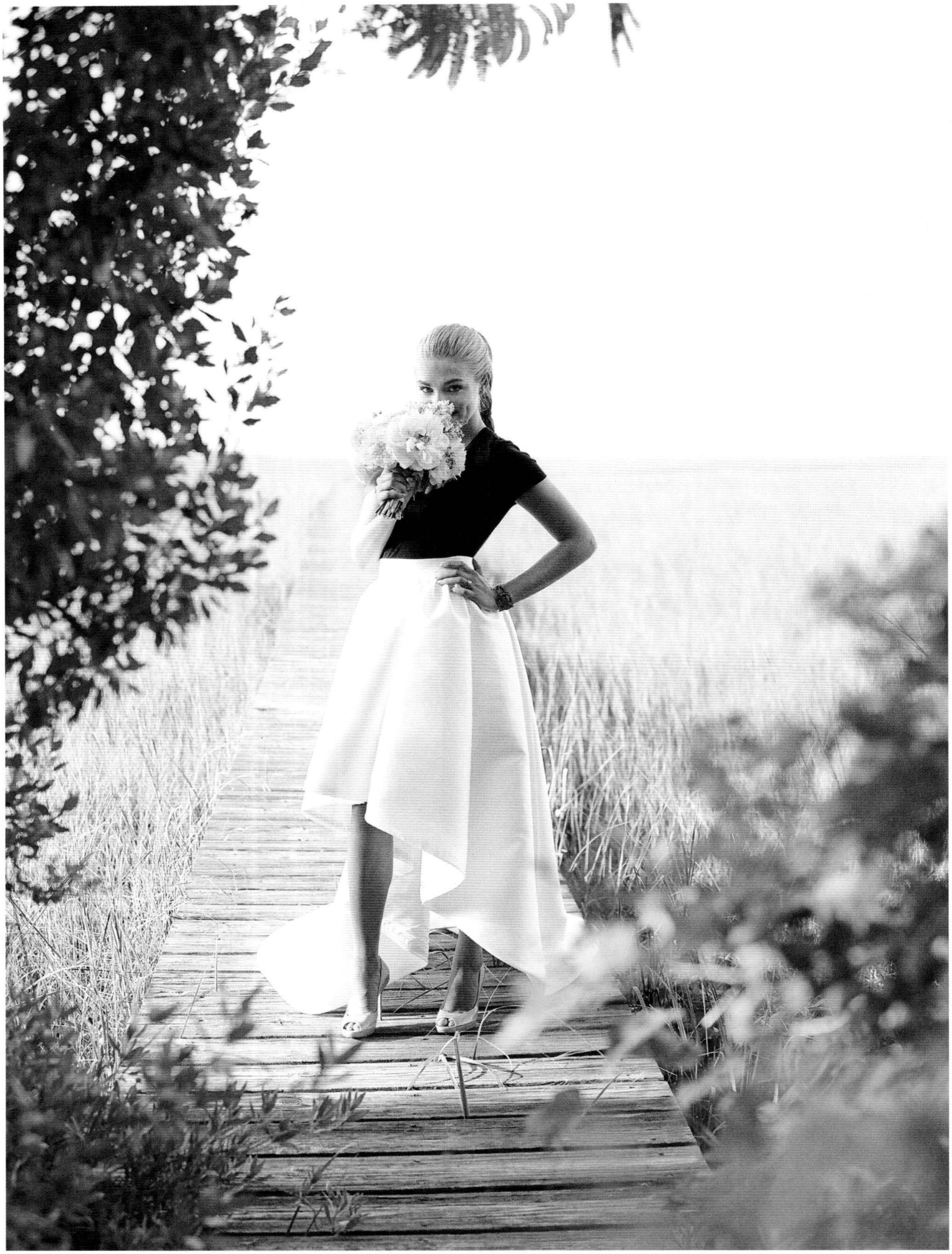

Set the table

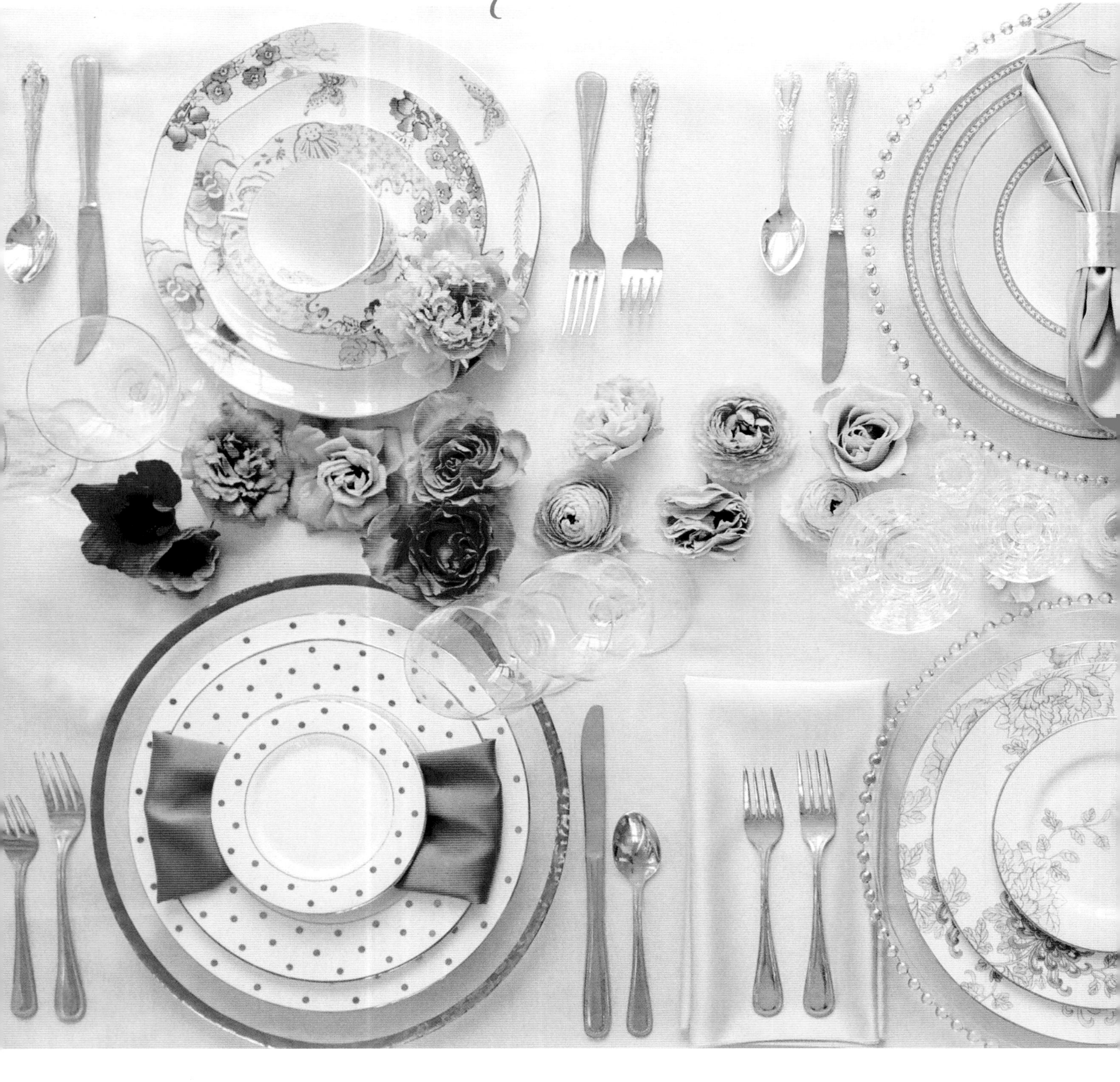

Flashback to cotillion? With formal place settings, each component presents opportunity for texture and design. There's no need to settle for typical; starting with your linen choice and working up through the charger, china, napkins, and flatware, complementary colors and unexpected patterns can create a balanced effect that wows.

KARA *and* JUSTIN

— HILTON HEAD, SC —

PHOTOGRAPHY BY DONNA VON BRUENING
SPENCER SPECIAL EVENTS
COLLETON RIVER PLANTATION CLUB

For Maryland-native Kara Colnitis and Iowa-native Justin Pudenz, enchanting Hilton Head held an instant allure when planning their May affair. Having grown up visiting the island, Kara planned an al fresco weekend inspired by the natural beauty of the Spanish moss and Colleton River—symbolized by a striking Palmetto emblem used throughout the décor. Soft gold and cream swathed the ceremony and reception, from the textured tent ceiling to the lush peonies adorning the bouquets and tabletops, while pops of coral added a playfulness to reflect Kara and Justin's lively relationship. The guests' experience, though, drove every decision, from the Atlanta-based band that kept everyone on the dance floor all night to the fireworks that dotted the sky during the couple's unforgettable farewell.

"I didn't want the reception to end, but little did Justin and I know that my mom had worked with Amanda Spencer to have fireworks shoot up as our car drove off and we left the reception. It was the icing on the cake to the best day of my life!"

IN ATTENDANCE

MOUNTAIN GRACE

 ARTISTA CAKES
Cake

 ASHEVILLE EVENT COMPANY, CORTNEY HAMLIN JACKSON
Design & Coordination

 BHLDN
Gown (200)

 CHARLOT ANNE JACKSON, CAROLINE JACKSON & EDWARD JENNINGS
Flower Girls & Ring Bearer

 FLOWERS BY LARRY
Floral Design

 IVY COOPER
Hair

 J MAJOR'S BRIDAL BOUTIQUE
Veil (200) and Jewelry

 LONESOME VALLEY & CANYON KITCHEN
Venue & Catering

 MELISSA GRIFFIN PAPPAS
Model

 PERRY VAILE PHOTOGRAPHY
Photography

PHOTOVISION
Film Processing

 POP OF COLOR
Makeup

ROWE HAMLIN INTERIORS
Décor Rental

 SABLE & GRAY PAPER CO.
Stationery

SARAH SEVEN
Gown (202)

WHITE BY VERA WANG
Veil (206)

LOWCOUNTRY VOW

Indie Film Lab, Film Processing

Ivana Krejci from Ivory & Beau, Gown

Jaclyn Jordan NYC, Veil

Michelle Royal, Hair & Makeup

Sarah Ingram, Floral Design & Calligraphy

Sawyer Baird, Photography

Sawyer Greenberg, Model

Twigs & Honey, Headpiece

AMANDA & HARRISON

Amanda Ghent & Company, String Quartet

Dave Prescott, DJ

Dinobrite Productions, Cinematography

Hightower Hall, Venue

Jeff Nash, Clergy

Jim Hjelm from Jo-Lin's Bridal, Gown

Liz Miller, Hair

Leroy Springs, Catering

Periwinkle Café & Bakery, Cake

Ribald Farm Nursery and Florist, Floral Design & Event Design

Sweet Carolina Weddings, Page Anderson, Wedding Design

Sylvan's, Rings

The Men's Shop, Tuxedos

Vince Lanier, Makeup

We Are the Hoffmans, Photography

Wedding Paper Divas, Stationery

MOUNTAIN GRACE

Retreat to Cashiers for nuptials steeped in tradition and natural beauty. Etheral lace, softly blooming wildflowers, and dainty delicacies fulfill a British-inspired dream.

Perry Vaile Photography
Asheville Event Company
Cashiers, NC

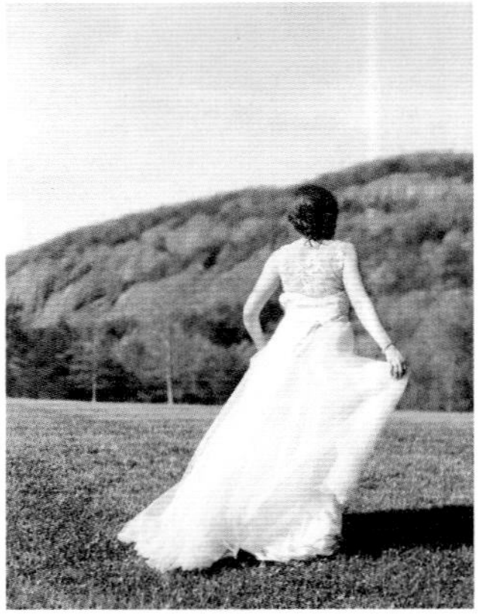
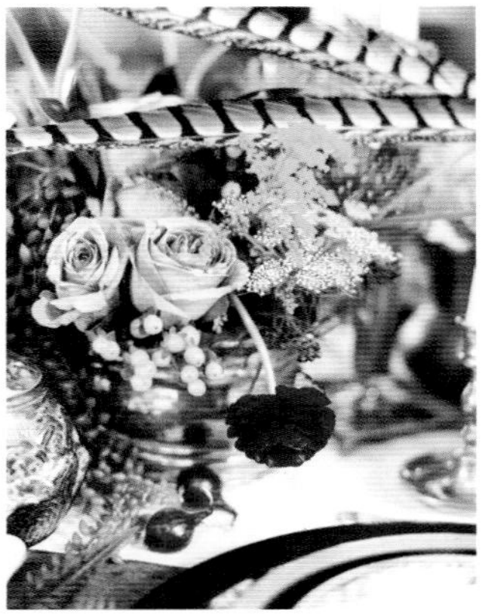
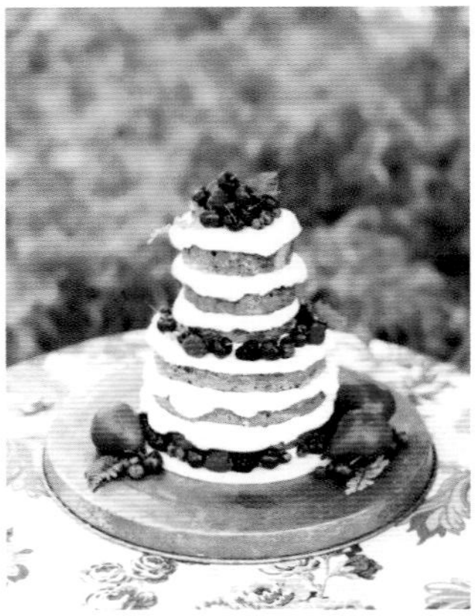
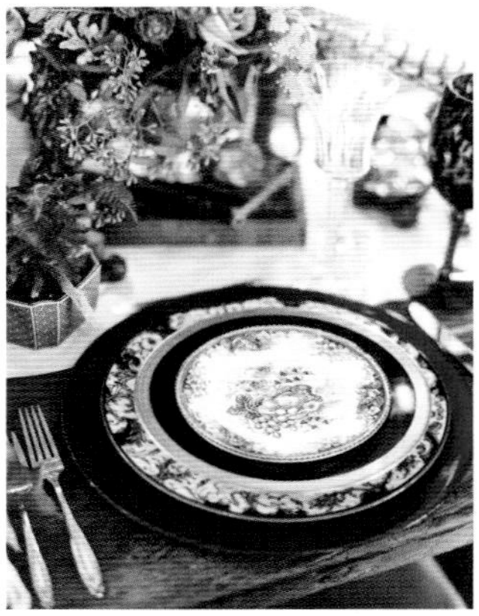
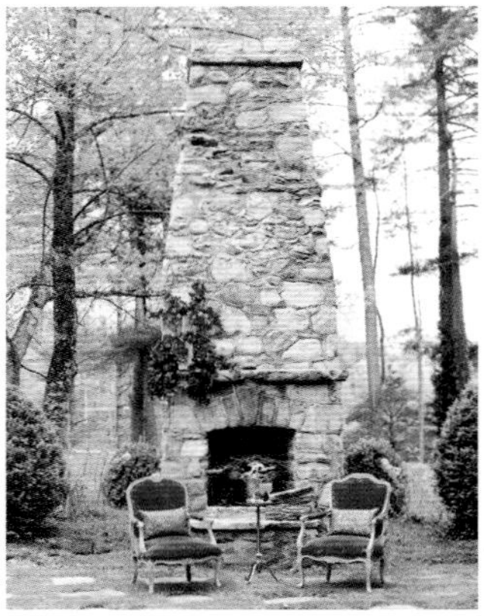
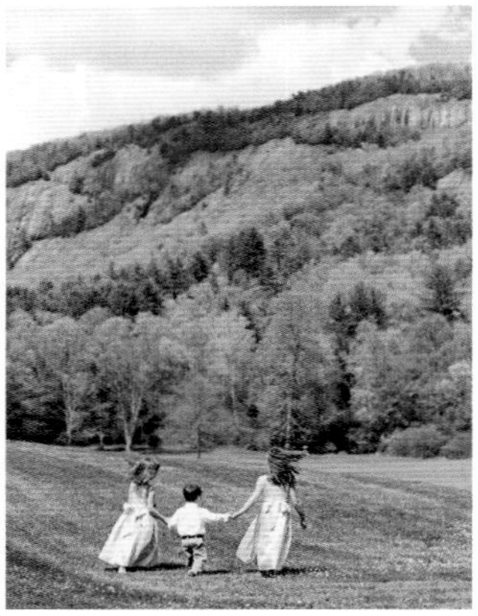
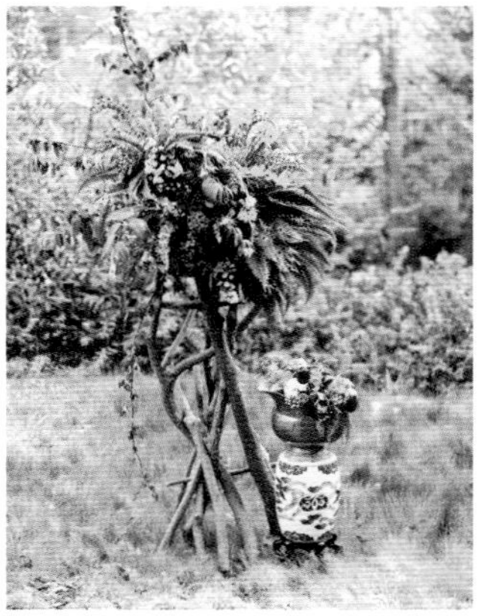
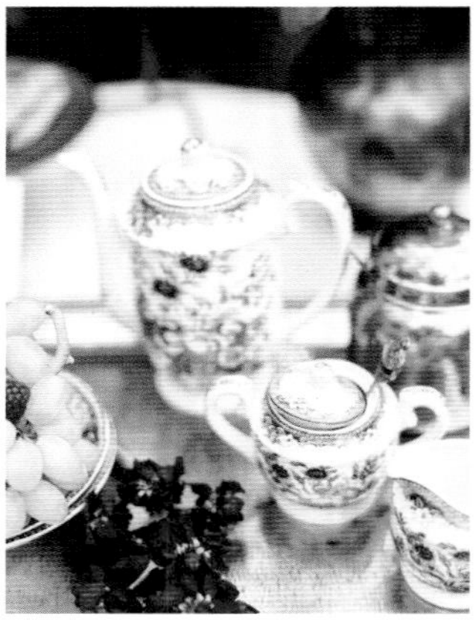
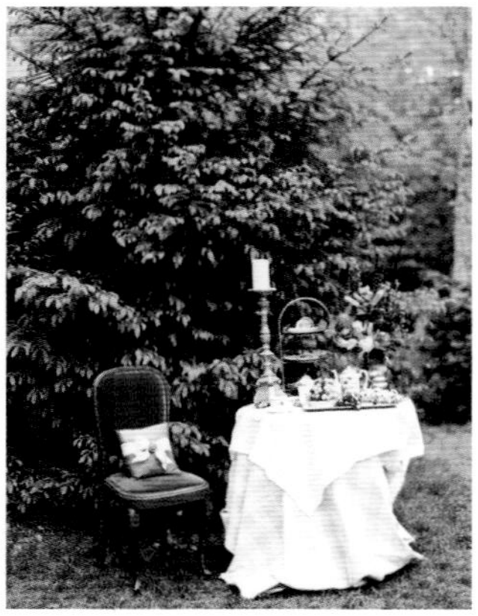
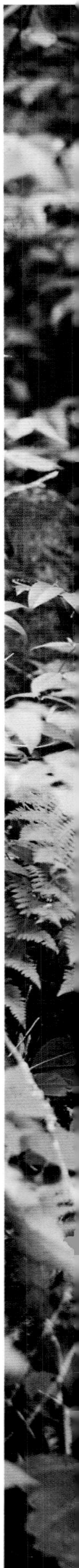

Lowcountry Vow

Photography by Sawyer Baird

Savannah, Ga.

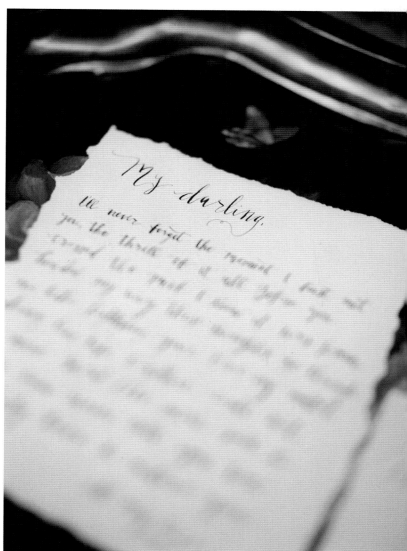

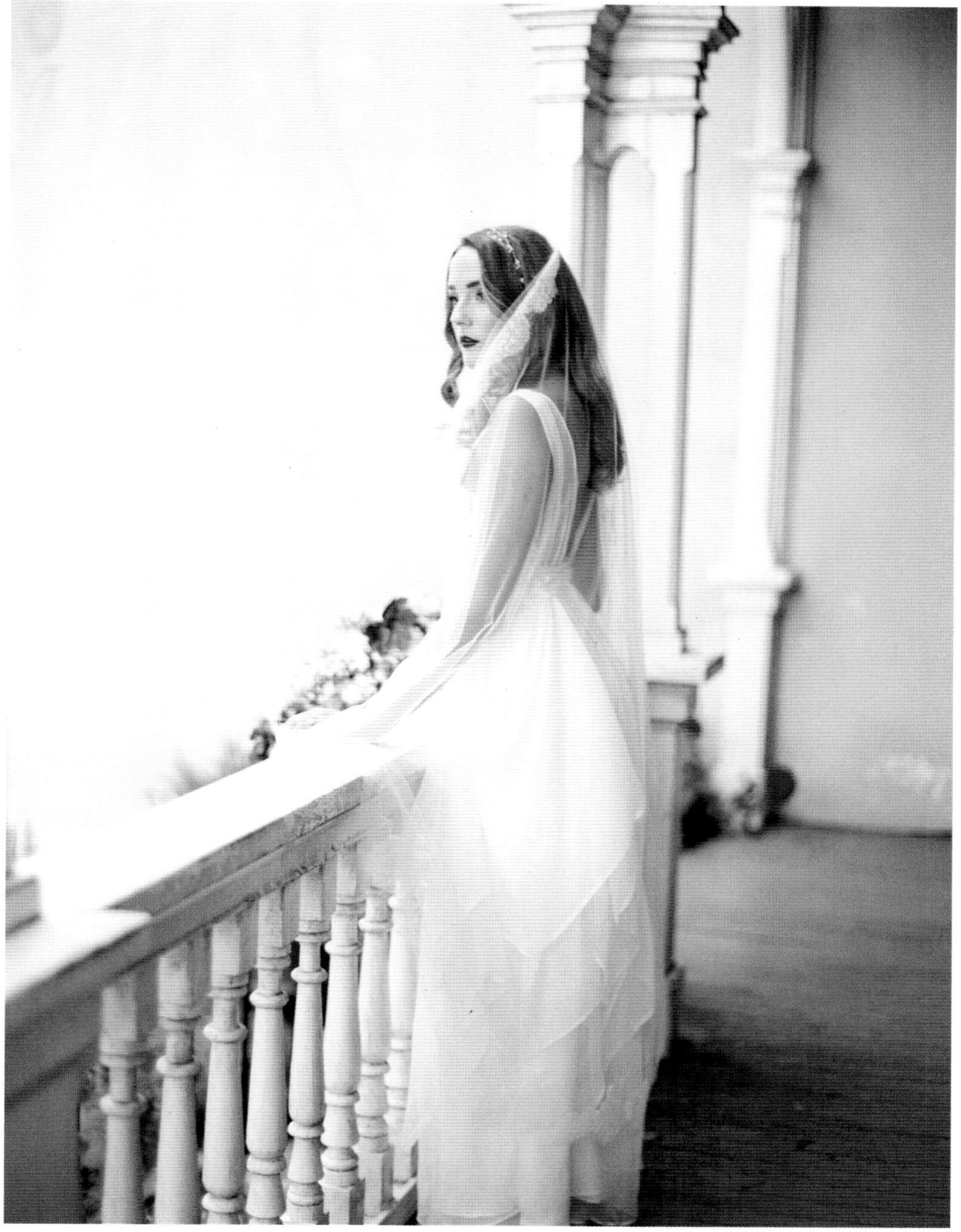

AMANDA *and* HARRISON

MCCONNELLS, SC

PHOTOGRAPHY BY WE ARE THE HOFFMANS

SWEET CAROLINA WEDDINGS
& RIBALD NURSERY & FLORIST

HIGHTOWER HALL

On a March day in McConnells, South Carolina, Amanda Jennings and Harrison Miller came together for a first look—and a sweet exchange of vows—under the great oak at Hightower Hall. It was only fitting that they choose a locale rich in Carolina history (the hall dates back to 1856), as they infused their own heritage throughout the day. The rustic wood elements at the ceremony site weren't chosen simply as décor—all of the logs were taken from the bride's grandfather's farm. With her mother's engagement ring and her grandmother's wedding band attached to her bouquet, Amanda walked down the aisle to the altar, draped in hallowed white, to join hands with Harrison, who would slip on his late grandfather's wedding band.

"When we first saw each other, I can still remember
exactly how I felt. I was so excited I was laughing,
and then immediately started crying, and he was
crying... And it was so, so special."

IN ATTENDANCE

 ASHLEY BABER WEDDINGS, ERICA STAWICK

Wedding Design

 AUBRE'S BRIDAL

Jewelry (223, necklace & 226, bracelet)

 BEVELLO

Attendant's Dress

 CHEESECAKE ETC.

Cake

 CLAIRE KUHLKIN

Model, Bride

 HARWELL PHOTOGRAPHY, JEREMY HARWELL

Photography

 HAYLEY KUHLKIN

Model, Attendant

EXQUISITE ELOPEMENT

 MORGAN KOUKOPOULOS

Model, Officiant

 MYERS MCKENZIE

Hair

 NECTAR FLORAL DESIGNS

Floral Design

 OLIVE PAPER

Stationery

 PAGE6 BOUTIQUE

Jewelry

 PARKER THOMAS

Model, Groom

 PARTY REFLECTIONS

Linens, China & Flatware

 PAUL SIMON CO.

Groom's Attire

 SAREH NOURI

Gown (224)

 TERI-LYN MAKEUP ARTIST

Makeup

 THE CLIFFS AT GLASSY & THE CLIFFS AT KEOWEE VINEYARDS

Venues

 THE LILY ROSE

Veil & Jewelry

 WATTERS FROM THE LILY ROSE

Gown (222)

 WTOO FROM THE LILY ROSE

Gown (226)

DELECTABLE CONFECTION

Anna Naphtali, Styling
Corbin Gurkin, Photography
Got What It Cakes, Cake (First and Fourth)
Hey Love! Events, Buffet
Separk Mansion, Venue
Sky's the Limit Bridal Sweets, Cake
(Second and Third)
Wow Factor Cakes, Cake (Fifth)

WHITLEY & DARIAN

Adorn Studio, Hair
Badgley Mischka, Shoes
Brakefield at Riverwalk, Venue
Brian Bunn Films, Cinematography
Charlotte Strings for Events, Musicians
Connie Duglin Specialty Linen & Chair Cover Rental, Rentals
Jasmine Howard, Makeup for Wedding
Karat Patch Jewelry, Engagement Ring
Lauren Rosenau Photography, Photography

Mortiz Reutch, Wedding Rings
New Creations Flower Company, Flowers
Olive Paper, Stationery
Party Tables, Rentals
Rev. Clifford Jones, Clergy
Royal Rides, Transportation
Shutterbooth, Photo Booth
Something Classic Catering, Catering
Split Second Sound, Entertainment
Sterling Event Design Group, Draping
Sweet Southern Glam, Makeup for Portraits
The Graceful Host, Wedding Design
Vera Wang, Bridesmaids' Dresses and Tuxedos
Victor Harper Couture from Nitsa's, Gown
Wow Factor Cakes, Cake

HEATHER & ROBERT

Carolina Herrera from Alexia's Bridal, Gown
Carolina Livery, Transportation
Ceremony Salon, Hair
Cinda's Creative Cakes, Cake
Graham Terhune Photography, Photography
Hot Dog Photo Booth, Photo Booth
Life Stage Films, Cinematography
Party Reflections, Rentals
Ply, Stationery
Private Residence, Reception Venue
Rev. Bob Dunham and Rev. Ernie Thompson, Clergy
Ruth Ross and Karen Havighurst, Wedding Planners
Sleeping Booty via East Coast Entertainment, Band
The Makeup Culture, Makeup
Theme Works, Rentals
Total Production Services, Lighting
University Presbyterian Church, Ceremony
Valentino, Shoes
Watered Garden, Floral Design

EXQUISITE ELOPEMENT

Steal away to the breathtaking Cliffs for an elopement with blushing details and sweeter-than-honey moments. Exchange your vows in a hushed chapel before embarking on your new adventure.

Harwell Photography
Ashley Baber Weddings
Landrum, SC

WHITLEY *and* DARIAN

FORT MILL, SC

LAUREN ROSENAU PHOTOGRAPHY
THE GRACEFUL HOST
BRAKEFIELD AT RIVERWALK

Whitley Saxton was born and raised in uptown Charlotte and met future groom Darian Stewart while out in the city with friends. So when Darian dropped to one knee in a SouthPark restaurant to pop the question, there was no doubt they would wed near the Queen City. The pair jumped into planning, and with the help of designer Ashley Cash, fell in love with Brakefield at Riverwalk on the Catawba River.

Their classic event, with a chic color palette of charcoal and ivory, showcased their love of the South with family and friends—with a fun twist. The bride and groom wanted to emulate the "party feel" of their first meeting, so the DJs of Split Second Sound kept the dance floor full all night long after a feast of traditional comfort foods like macaroni and cheese and fried chicken bites.

"With Darian's career [in the NFL], we move around a lot. We met in Charlotte, moved to St. Louis, and now we're in Baltimore. We were most looking forward to the stability of something being truly official."

Delectable confection

Celebrate your sweet new love with the traditional ritual of the wedding cake. Whether you opt for classic white-on-white texture or something a bit more whimsical, the flavors, hues, and design should all complement other elements of your décor. The cake presents opportunity for newlywed bliss, too—by choosing a different flavor for each tier, compromise is as easy as pie.

HEATHER *and* ROBERT

GRAHAM TERHUNE PHOTOGRAPHY
PRIVATE RESIDENCE

*W*hen bride Heather Kileff walked down the aisle toward her groom Robert Hutchins, it was the blend of old and new that created such an emotionally charged moment. The "Triumphal March" from *Aida* echoed throughout the historic church, conjuring the walks of three women in Heather's family who also chose the revered processional. Both Heather's and Robert's childhood ministers awaited them at the altar to officiate and bless the marriage. Even Heather's style, an effortless blend of modern *mode* and timeless elegance, spoke to her desire for nuptials both traditional and fresh. After a perfect day in pinks and grays, the two again chose an unexpected path, jetting off to honeymoon on a South African safari.

"After the wedding, we had the biggest, cheesiest smiles.
It was so exciting walking down that aisle—we were
on a giddy adrenaline high. We took pictures with
the photographers in the courtyard of the church.
Relieved, in disbelief, and so happy."

IN ATTENDANCE

CONTENTS

Anna Naphtali
Photography

Studio Cultivate
*Floral Design &
Installation*

FOREWORD

Sofia
Negron Photography
Photography

INTRODUCTION

220 North Tryon at
Foundation For The
Carolinas
Venue

Be Pretty
Hair & Makeup

Come+Together Events
Event Design

Diamonds Direct
SouthPark
Jewelry

Erin Grey Couture
Gowns

J Major's Bridal Boutique
Wardrobe

Jessica Boyd,
Karen Edmundson,
Ashley Ehmann &
Gabrielle Glenn
Models

Kristin Vining
Photography
*Creative Direction
& Photography*

La-tea-da's Catering
Specialty Drinks

Lazaro
Noir Bridesmaid Dress

Lucy & Company
Butterfly Chair

Nina
Clutches

Party Tables
Linen & Draping

Romare Bearden Park
Exterior Venue

San Patrick
Gray Bridesmaid Dress

The Bloom Room
Floral Design

The Dunhill Hotel
Styling Suite

West Elm
Bar Cart & Coffee Table

**FRONT & BACK
COVER**

Dréa Cunningham,
Photo Artist
Photography

Anna Wolf
Model

Ashley Brook Perryman
Hair & Makeup

Carolyn Shepard Design
Group
Floral Design

Cheryl King Couture
Pillbox Hat & Jewelry

Erin Grey Couture
Gown

**INSIDE FRONT
COVER &
TITLE PAGE**

Abany Bauer
Styling & Flowers

Gossamer
Gown

Heather Payne
Photography
Photography

INSIDE BACK COVER

Gossamer
Gown

Laura Gordon
Photography
Photography

Photovision
Film Processing

**AUTHOR
HEADSHOTS**

Be Pretty,
Lindsey Regan Thorne
Hair & Makeup

Crystal Stokes
Photography
Photo of Miss Wilson

Kristin Vining
Photography
*Photo of
Miss Humphries*

Neiman Marcus
Miss Wilson's wardrobe

The Lily Rose
Miss Humphries' wardrobe

Since the very first moments of this crazy book idea, it's the art of weddings that has driven every decision. We are continually inspired by the incredible professionals in our region and across the country who contributed to these pages. The artistry, creativity, and passion displayed by each one is a true representation of the Southern spirit. So first and foremost, we send our gratitude to everyone who had faith in a bold idea and shared their time and expertise with us.

We'd also like to thank the small army of folks who have supported us and lifted this dream of ours for the last two years. Everyone who helped brainstorm shoot ideas, weighed in on photo choices, or simply brought us coffee (bless you!) on late work nights—of those, we each thank our parents most of all.

Lastly, we owe the completion of this work to the Carolina brides (and brides in spirit) who cherish our dear magazine. The *Carolina Bride* brand is just shy of its 25th birthday, and it's the readers that bring the deepest joy and satisfaction to our work. This is for you all.

-CRISTINA & DREW

PHOTO BY Anna Naphtali